Understanding 1-2 Thessalonians

An Examination

But now being made free from sin, and become
servants to God, you have your fruit unto holiness,
and the end everlasting life.

For we preach not ourselves, but Christ Jesus the
Lord; and ourselves your servants for Jesus' sake. For
God, who commanded the light to shine out of
darkness,
Has shined in our hearts, to give the light of
the knowledge of the glory of God
in the face of Jesus Christ.

For all who love the LORD Jesus Christ,
desire to understand the Scriptures,
and look for the blessed hope
of His glorious appearing.

Amen.

Understanding 1-2 Thessalonians

An Examination

By

Don Samdahl

Thy word is a lamp unto my feet,
And a light unto my path.
Psalm 119.105

A Doctrine Publication
Doctrine.org

New Testament quotations are from the author's
The New Testament Study Bible (BDV).
Old Testament quotations are from the KJV
with updated language.

First Edition: 2023
Printed in the United States of America
ISBN: 978-1-958366-02-8

Table of Contents

Framework of Gods Programs Through the Ages

Program	Mankind	Israel	Church	Israel Redux	Kingdom	New Heavens and New Earth
Key Figure	Adam	Abraham	Paul	Antichrist	Christ	God the Father
Length	Adam to Abraham	Abraham to Paul	Paul to Rapture	7 Years	1,000 Years	Eternal
Revelation	Revealed by the Prophets		Unrevealed by the Prophets	Revealed by the Prophets		

A detailed chart is at doctrine.org/chart-of-gods-programs

Preface

As a general introduction to the Thessalonians letters, three details are noteworthy. The first is that the Thessalonian letters were Paul's first letters, written shortly after the Jerusalem Council, after the question of the gospel and Gentile salvation was settled.

The second element of note is that these letters reveal two of Paul's secrets, those revelations he received from the ascended Lord. The first secret was the gospel of grace, Paul's gospel. Such a statement may startle the reader about Paul's gospel being a secret. Was it really a secret? Paul wrote the Ephesians, which most of Christendom seems not to know:

> [18] Through every prayer and request, pray at all times in *the* Spirit, even for this very thing, watching with all perseverance and request for all the saints, [19] and for me, so I might be given *a* message with boldness in opening my mouth, to make known the secret of the gospel, [20] for which I am *an* ambassador in *a* chain, so by it I might be bold to speak as I must (Ephesians 6.18-19).

The gospel Paul proclaimed was unknown before the ascended Lord revealed it to him (Galatians 1.11-12). It was because of Paul's gospel that the Jerusalem Council of Acts 15 had to be held. In Paul's account of the meeting, he wrote he had to explain his gospel to the Twelve and the others at that council (Galatians 2.2). Had they known Paul's gospel, this would have been unnecessary. Indeed, had they understood Paul's gospel, there would have been no argument about Gentile salvation and no need for a council.

The other secret in these letters, their chief subject, is the Pre-Tribulation Rapture. Paul later wrote the Corinthians that the Pre-Tribulation Rapture was a secret:

> [51] Behold! I tell you *a* secret: we will not all sleep[1] but we will all be changed— [52] in *an* instant, in *the* blink of *an* eye, at the last trumpet. For *the* trumpet will sound and the dead will be raised incorruptible. Then, we will be changed. [53] For this corruptible *body* must put on incorruption and this mortal must put on immortality (1 Corinthians 15.51-53).

The final detail to note, unique to Paul's letters, is that Paul placed the Thessalonians under an oath before the Lord to read 1 Thessalonians to "all the holy brethren" (1 Thessalonians 5.27). No other book or letter carries such a charge. This command shows how important Paul viewed teaching the Pre-Tribulation Rapture, our "blessed hope."

LEXINGTON, VIRGINIA, 2023

---

[1] That is, "die."

Introduction to 1 Thessalonians

Written about 52 A.D., 1 Thessalonians was Paul's first letter, the first penned record of Church doctrine. Paul wrote the letter from Corinth, not Athens, as some manuscripts have, for Silas and Timothy had rejoined him (1 Thessalonians 1.1; Acts 18.1, 5). Paul, Silas, Timothy, and Luke (always in the background) began the Thessalonians church. Luke narrated how they came to Greece as a result of Paul's Macedonian vision (Acts 16.6-10) and travelled through the Greek cities of Philippi, Amphipolis, and Apollonia until they reached Thessalonica (Acts 16.11-17.1).

Paul wrote no letters until after the Council of Jerusalem. Why? That council settled the question of the gospel and the matter of Gentile salvation. Even more, with Peter's statement (Acts 15.11), Paul's gospel became the sole message of salvation for both Jew and Gentile. It supplanted the gospel of the kingdom, which began with John the Baptist and continued in Jesus' earthly ministry and the ministry of the Twelve. The focus of the gospel of the kingdom was Christ's *identity*, who He was. This is clear from the salvation accounts of Peter, Nathaniel, Martha, the Samaritan woman at the well, and the Ethiopian Phillip met on the road to Gaza. In contrast, Paul's gospel focused on Christ's *work*—He died for our sins and rose from the dead (1 Corinthians 15.1-4).

As a result of Peter's pronouncement at the Council of Jerusalem, Paul could write that any who proclaimed a gospel different from his was cursed (Galatians 1.6-9). Paul's gospel will continue as the message of salvation until God completes His Church and removes it from the earth. After this, the gospel of the kingdom will return and be the message of salvation in God's prophetic program (Matthew 24.14) during the Tribulation, God's wrath, known also as the Day of the Lord, and Daniel's seventieth week (Daniel 9.24-27). Sixty-nine weeks have passed and one week remains in God's prophetic program, the seven-year

Tribulation. The Day of the Lord was the great theme of Israel's prophets—God's wrath against mankind, Christ's return, and His reign on earth.

Prominent in his two letters to the Thessalonians, especially his first letter, is Paul's gospel (1 Thessalonians 1.5, 2.2, 4, 8-9, 3.2; 2 Thessalonians 2.14) and the doctrine of the Pre-Tribulational Rapture. The Pre-Tribulational Rapture was the first Church doctrine Paul taught the Thessalonians after they believed the gospel. Why was this?

Paul thought the Lord would soon complete His Church and remove it. God would then wrap up His prophetic program concerning Israel and the Gentiles with the Tribulation and Christ's advent at its end. Paul expected the Rapture to occur in his lifetime and wanted the Thessalonians to understand and anticipate this great event. Second, the Pre-Tribulational Rapture is the Church's "blessed hope" (Titus 2.13), our resurrection, when God will resurrect the bodies of members of the Church who have died and change the mortal bodies of members of the Church who are alive to eternal, immortal bodies. The Rapture is the last stage of salvation of believers who comprise the Church, the redemption of our bodies. Paul regarded this as the greatest doctrine of the Church after the gospel. Thus, he *commanded* the Church to teach the Pre-Tribulation Rapture.

All ancient manuscripts have the same order of Paul's seven letters to churches (Romans through Thessalonians). Paul's Thessalonian letters are his first letters, chronologically. Doctrinally, Romans is first. Doctrinally, Thessalonians is last for the Rapture, the main message of the Thessalonian letters, completes the Church's salvation—our resurrection.

The Thessalonian embrace of God's word encouraged further missionary operations in southern and northern Greece, Achaia and Macedonia (1 Thessalonians 1.8). These believers were a model church, an example to other believers and Paul wrote them joyfully due to the good report he received from Timothy of their faith and love (1 Thessalonians 3.6).

No Church truth has undergone greater attack than the Pre-Tribulational Rapture. Its vigorous enemies are in seminaries, pulpits, and Sunday schools. Those who attack it have little understanding of God's strategic plan, unable to distinguish between the Church and Israel, between God's prophetic program for Israel and the Gentiles and His secret program of the Church, the body of Christ. They do understand Paul's doctrines for they do not recognize his unique apostleship—not as an extension of the Twelve but Christ's handpicked agent to found the Church and reveal all its doctrines. As a result, confusion reigns in Christendom. The goal of this commentary is to mend this wound and reveal the great truth of the Pre-Tribulation Rapture, the Church's "blessed hope."

1 Thessalonians

---

1 Thessalonians 1

Greetings and Praise

1 Paul, and Silvanus, and Timothy to the church of *the*
Thessalonians in God *the* Father and *the* Lord Jesus
Christ: Grace to you and peace from God our Father,
and *the* Lord Jesus Christ![1]
2 We thank the God always for you all as we mention
you in our prayers,
3 by unceasingly remembering your work of the faith
and the labor of the love, and the endurance of the hope
of our Lord Jesus Christ, in the presence of our God
and Father,
4 because we know, beloved brethren, your election by
the God.
5 For our gospel did not come to you in word only, but
also in power and in *the* Holy Spirit, and in much
assurance, as you know how we acted among you for
your sakes.

Comment:

Verses 1-5: Paul, Silvanus, and Timothy founded the church at Thessalonica during Paul's second missionary journey (Acts 17.1-4). This letter was a follow-up to encourage them and to reiterate the doctrines Paul had taught them. Silvanus, Σιλουανός, "Woody," was the Latinized form of the Hebrew name Silas, what Luke called him.[2] Paul wrote to "the church of *the* Thessalonians in God *the* Father and *the* Lord Jesus Christ (verse 1). Such designation describes a

---

[1] Some manuscripts do not have ἀπὸ Θεοῦ πατρὸς ἡμῶν καὶ κυρίου Ἰησοῦ Χριστοῦ "from God our Father and the Lord Jesus Christ."
[2] Luke's use of Silvanus, his Jewish name, Silas, is evidence Luke was Jewish.

true church—one in God the Father and the Lord Jesus Christ.

The noun translated "church," ἐκκλησία, must be understood according to context. Here it means members of the Church, the body of Christ. Generally, the noun ἐκκλησία denotes a group of people. For example, in Acts 19, ἐκκλησία is found three times, in verses 32, 39, and 41. Each has a different sense. In verse 32 it means "mob," in verse 39, "court," and in verse 41, "crowd." When ἐκκλησία is found in writings directed to Jews, it means Jews who had believed the gospel of the kingdom (cf. Hebrews 2.12, 12.23; James 5.14; 3 John 1.6, 9-10; Revelation 1.4, 11, 20, 2.1, 2.7-8, 11-12, 17-18, 23, 29, 3.1, 6-7, 13-14, 22, 22.16). When Paul used the term, it usually meant members of the Church, the body of Christ, those who had believed his gospel, the gospel of the grace of God (1 Corinthians 15.1-4). Context controls the meaning of the word.

Acts records how Paul, with Silas (Barnabas' replacement), went to Greece after Paul received his Macedonian vision (Acts 16.6-10). At Philippi, Lydia was saved. After this, Paul and Silas were beaten and imprisoned for expelling a demon, a spirit of Python,[3] from a young woman. At midnight in the prison, God caused an earthquake and the jailer was saved. After Paul and Silas were released from jail, they travelled through Amphipolis and Apollonia where they came to Thessalonica (Acts 17.1). While there, they taught in the synagogue for three sabbaths, about three weeks (Acts 17.2-3).

A normal, as opposed to a special sabbath, is the seventh day of the week from Friday sundown to Saturday sundown. But it appears Paul stayed longer with the Thessalonians than three weeks from passages such as 1 Thessalonians 2.9, 2 Thessalonians 3.8, and Philippians 4.16. Luke's focus was primarily on Jewish matters since his primary purpose in writing

---

[3] In Greek mythology, "Python," Πύθων, was the snake or dragon that guarded the oracle at Delphi, located in upper, central Greece near Mt. Parnassus.

Acts was to explain to Jews why the kingdom of God did not come.

Unlike other letters in which Paul identified himself as "apostle," ἀπόστολος, the title is absent in both Thessalonian letters. Why? One reason may have been that as his first letters, he did not think he needed to use this title since he founded the Thessalonian church and they knew him. Another is no serious problems attended this church and Paul did not think he needed to make a strong authoritative point of apostleship. He used the designation "apostle" to the Romans because they had never met him—they knew him only by reputation. The Galatian, Corinthian, and Colossian churches had significant problems and Paul used his title to assert his apostolic authority. The letters to Timothy and Titus while personal, would be used for doctrine, so Paul included the title as gravitas. Paul did not use "apostle" to Philemon for he was making a personal appeal about Onesimus.

Paul wished these believers "grace and peace from God our Father, and *the* Lord Jesus Christ." This greeting characterizes all of Paul's letters to the Church. While Peter and John used the expression "grace and peace" (1 Peter 1.2 2 Peter 1.2; 2 John 1.3; Revelation 1.4) also, Paul's use of the phrase was theologically significant for his ministry as the apostle of grace and founder of the Church, the body of Christ.

According to God's prophetic plan, represented and proclaimed by Peter and John, God would execute wrath on the earth following rejection of His Son (Psalm 2.1-5; 110.1). But instead, God extended grace and peace and saved Paul to begin the Church. God's grace and peace became displayed fully through the revelations the risen Lord gave Paul, especially His revelation of how His salvation was for *all* by faith *alone* through his gospel (1 Corinthians 15.1-4). As such, grace and peace should be the hallmark of every church wishing to obey Christ.

In verses 2-4, Paul thanked God for the Thessalonians, remembering their work of "the faith," τῆς πίστεως, the labor of "the love," τῆς ἀγάπης, and the endurance of "the hope," τῆς ἐλπίδος, of our Lord Jesus Christ, in the presence of our God and Father. The articular nouns and genitives of result denote the Thessalonians work that resulted from the faith, Paul's doctrines, the work as a result of the love, the love that results from Paul's doctrines, and the endurance that comes from the hope, the resurrection of members of the Church, Paul's doctrine of the Pre-Tribulation Rapture.

Paul wrote the Corinthians that the sign gifts of languages, prophecy, and knowledge would soon pass but faith, hope, and love would remain (1 Corinthians 13). After Paul received all Church doctrine from the Lord sign gifts disappeared and faith, hope, and love continued. As such, unlike sign gifts, Paul mentioned them throughout his letters after Corinthians.

Paul declared the Lord Jesus Christ is now in the presence of God the Father (verse 3). Many passages declare He is seated at His Father's right hand (Matthew 22.44, 26:64; Mark 12.36, 14.62, 16.19; Luke 20.42, 22.69; Acts 2.25, 33-34; Romans 8.34; Ephesians 1.20; Colossians 3.1; Hebrews 1.3, 13, 8.1, 10.12, 12.2; 1 Peter 3.22). These passages cite Psalm 110.1, the most quoted Old Testament verse in the New Testament. According to God's prophetic plan with Israel and the nations, Christ will continue to sit at His Father right hand until He returns to destroy His enemies and set up His throne in Jerusalem and rule earth (Zechariah 14.9; cf. Psalm 2.6)

Paul closed the thought of thanking God "because we know, beloved brethren, your election by the God." This is the only time Paul used the noun "election," ἐκλογή, for members of the Church. He used it four times for Israel (cf. Romans 9.11, 11:5, 7, 28). Theologically, "election" is equal to "calling," κλητός, (Romans 1.1, 6-7, 8.28; 1 Corinthians 1.1-2, 24).

Paul explained in Romans 8.29-30 that God's foreknowledge governs His predestining, calling, declaring righteous, and glorifying. God knows everything, from beginning to end. Since He is outside time, past, present, and future are "now." He can see everything as present. Since we are "inside time," we describe God "foreseeing" or "foreknowing." God knows how a person will respond to Him and this knowledge governs predestining, calling, justifying, and glorifying.

On the basis of God's foreknowledge, the Scriptures declare members of the Church, the body of Christ, have been chosen (ἐκλέγομαι) "before the foundation of the world," πρὸ καταβολῆς κόσμου (Ephesians 1.4). *Precisely* how the divine and human wills cooperate in salvation is a mystery the Scriptures do not reveal. What they reveal is that whoever believes in Christ, calls on Him, will be saved (John 11.26, 12.46; Acts 2.21; Romans 10.11, 13; Revelation 22.17). God has provided salvation for everyone but His salvation only benefits those who want it. He is no tyrant.

In verse 5, Paul reminded the Thessalonians that his gospel, "our gospel," τὸ εὐαγγέλιον ἡμῶν, did not come to them in word alone but in power and by the Holy Spirit. No miracles are mentioned in the Thessalonian letters. God's greatest power is not miracles but His power to change lives through the gospel and the Holy Spirit. Paul wrote the Romans, "For I am not ashamed of the gospel of the Christ for it is *the* power of God (δύναμις θεοῦ) for salvation to everyone who believes: to Jew first and to Greek" (Romans 1.16). What did Paul mean by the phrase, "the gospel of the Christ," τὸ εὐαγγέλιον τοῦ Χριστοῦ? The expression is a genitive of source, the source of Paul's gospel was Christ. He wrote the Galatians,

> [11] Now I declare to you brethren, the gospel I proclaimed is not after man. [12] For I neither received nor was taught from man but through revelation of Jesus Christ (Galatians 1.11-12).

Paul received the gospel he proclaimed directly from the ascended Lord, the reason he called it "my gospel" (Romans 2.16, 16.25; 2 Corinthians 4.3; 2 Timothy 2.8). What is Paul's gospel? The clearest declaration is 1 Corinthians 15.1-4:

> [1] Now I declare to you, brethren, the gospel that I proclaimed to you, which you also received, by which also you stand, [2] through which also you are saved, if[4] you possess that message I proclaimed to you, unless you believed in vain. [3] For I delivered to you first what I also received: Christ died for our sins, according to the Scriptures, [4] and that He was buried, and that He has been raised on the third day, according to the Scriptures.

This was the gospel the Thessalonians believed for salvation. Salvation involves cooperation of the divine and human will. The human side is believing—believing Christ died for one's sins and rose from the dead for one's justification. The divine side is "in power and in the Holy Spirit" (verse 5) by which God draws a person to Himself through His word. Luke wrote the Lord opened Lydia's heart "to heed the things spoken by Paul" (Acts 16.14). Paul wrote the Romans, "So, the faith *is* from hearing but the hearing *is* through *the* word of God" (Romans 10.17). God wants all to be saved (1 Timothy 2.4) and none to perish (2 Peter 3.9) but forces Himself on no one. Every person has an equal opportunity for salvation and each person must choose.

In addition to the gospel coming in power and in the Holy Spirit, it came in "much assurance," πληροφορία, (verse 5), a word only Paul used (cf. Colossians 2.2; Hebrews 6.11, 10.22). This noun πληροφορία is linked with ἐν δυνάμει, "in power," and ἐν πνεύματι ἁγίῳ, "in (or by) the Holy Spirit." Paul's gospel was received with the full assurance that it was truth (cf. 1 Thessalonians 2.13).

Paul's statement, "as you know how we acted among you for your sakes" (verse 5) reminded them that he acted honorably and courteously towards them. Paul trusted in the power of the gospel and the Holy Spirit. How daunting it must have been for him and his companions to travel to foreign cities and unknown

---

[4] A 1st class condition where the reality is assumed true.

peoples. Everywhere Paul preached, opposition met his salvation message. But the source of his boldness, for which he prayed (Ephesians 6.19; Philippians 1.20; 1 Thessalonians 2.2), came from the glorified Christ.

No greater need exists in Christendom than for pastors and teachers to proclaim Paul's gospel, "the power of God for salvation to everyone who believes" (Romans 1.16). Paul wrote the Corinthians, that he proclaimed the gospel "not by wisdom of speech so that the cross of the Christ might not be nullified" (1 Corinthians 1.17). Greek and Roman orators were trained in various rhetorical devices to sway and persuade audiences. Such methods should never be used by those who proclaim God's word. Men and women are not drawn to Christ by oratorical techniques or theatrics but by clearly presenting God's word. God's word has the power and God's Spirit moves hearts to Christ.

Much confusion exists about the gospel. While the gospel is simple and straightforward, many add to it so that it becomes confusing. People are told to "invite Christ into their heart," "accept Jesus as their personal Savior," "repent and receive Christ," etc. Such messages are confusion, "strange fire" before God (Leviticus 10.1; Numbers 3.4, 26.61).

A Biblical presentation of salvation is that Christ died for one's sins and rose from the dead and that if one trusts in His work, one is saved from sin and death, forgiven, and given eternal life. Anything added to this creates confusion. We are to *believe* the gospel, not "invite" Christ, "accept" Christ, etc. As noted above, the clearest presentation of the gospel is 1 Corinthians 15.1-4, the message Paul gave the Thessalonians. They believed it and were saved (cf. 1 Thessalonians 4.14). Why make what God has made simple, complex? Why add to God's word? The gospel is the power of God for salvation to everyone who believes (Romans 1.16). God's Spirit works with *His* word, not *man's* word. God wishes all to be saved and will bring this to pass if we faithfully proclaim His salvation. We only have one responsibility: communicate the gospel as clearly and simply as possible. God does the rest.

---

6 And you became imitators of us, and of the Lord, for
you received the word in much affliction, with *the* joy
of *the* Holy Spirit,
7 so you became *an* example to all the believers in
Macedonia and Achaia.
8 For from you the word of the Lord has sounded forth,
not only in Macedonia and Achaia, but in every place.
Your faith toward the God has gone abroad so that we
do not have to say anything.
9 For they themselves report about how you welcomed
us and how you turned to the God from the idols to
serve *the* living and true God
10 and to wait for His Son from the heavens, whom He
raised from the dead, Jesus, the One who rescues us
from the coming wrath.

Comment:

Verses 6-10: In verse 6, Paul declared the Thessalonians became "imitators of us (μιμηταὶ ἡμῶν) and of the Lord." While "us" possibly referred to Paul, Silvanus, and Timothy, it is more likely a nosism and "us" meant Paul himself based on what Paul wrote elsewhere. Paul used the nouns μιμητής, συμμιμητής and the verb μιμέομαι[5] to urge believers to copy or imitate him. Consider the following passages:

1. Therefore, I urge you, become imitators (μιμηταί) of me (1 Corinthians 4.16).
2. Become imitators (μιμηταί) of me as I also am of Christ (1 Corinthians 11.1).
3. Become as I am because I also became as you brethren—I implore you (Galatians 4.12).
4. Brethren, become imitators (συμμιμηταί) of me and observe those who still so walk, as you have us for a pattern (τύπον) (Philippians 3.17).

---

[5] These words are the basis of words such as mimeograph, mimic, mimicry.

5. And you became imitators (μιμηταὶ) of us, and of the Lord, for you received the word in much affliction, with the joy of the Holy Spirit (1 Thessalonians 1.6).
6. For yourselves know how you must imitate (μιμεῖσθαι) us for we did not act disorderly among you (2 Thessalonians 3.7).
7. Not because we do not have the authority, but that we might give ourselves as an example (τύπον) for you to imitate (μιμεῖσθαι) us (2 Thessalonians 3.9).

Paul is the only Biblical writer who told believers to copy or imitate him. Why? The simple, but profound, answer is that Paul is the founder of the Church, the body of Christ, and all Church doctrine comes from his letters. No Church doctrine is found in the Gospels or the writings of James, Peter, John, or Jude. Those writings were to Jews saved through the gospel of the kingdom under God's covenant and prophetic program. The Church is outside God's covenant and prophetic program. This is a great truth almost no one in Christendom understands.

Paul wrote that the Church, the body of Christ, was a secret (Ephesians 3.1-13) the ascended Lord revealed to him. How is it so few know this when Paul plainly declared this? Why is Christendom so ignorant of Paul and Church theology?

Excursus: Did the Church Begin at Pentecost?

The vast majority in Christendom believe and teach the Church, the body of Christ, began at Pentecost, in Acts 2. The basis for this view presents the following logic: The Church is the body of Christ. Membership into the body of Christ is through the baptism of the Holy Spirit. The baptism of the Holy Spirit occurred at Pentecost. Therefore, the Church began at Pentecost. The above propositions appear reasoned and strong. But when the Scriptures themselves are examined, such logic collapses.

To see this, the Church must first be defined. The Church is that organism in which Jew and Gentile are baptized by the Holy Spirit, identified in Christ's death and resurrection, and indwelt by the Holy Spirit. Those so baptized and identified become part of "the body of Christ," a new creation. One acquires this new identity by faith alone, believing Paul's gospel, Christ died for one's sins and rose from the dead. This definition is based on Romans 3.22,24-25, 28, 4.4-5, 5.1, 6.3-6, 8.11; 1 Corinthians 3.16, 6.19, 12.12-27; 2 Corinthians 5.17; Galatians 3.27-28; Ephesians 1-22-23; Colossians 1.18, 3.11.

The following are twenty proofs from Acts that show conclusively the Church did not begin at Pentecost.

1. The coming of the Holy Spirit was a Jewish promise, the New Covenant, which promised forgiveness of sins and the indwelling Spirit to Jews (cf. Jeremiah 31.31-34; Ezekiel 11.16-20, 36.21-28; Joel 2.28-29). It was a covenant promise associated with God's regathering Jews into the promised land. Peter quoted Joel's prophecy (Acts 2.16-21) which stated the Spirit would be poured on "all flesh." The verses that follow qualify that "all flesh" do not mean "every person" but Jews—"your sons," "your daughters," "your old men," "your young men." None of the passages indicated the Holy Spirit coming on Gentiles.
2. Pentecost was a Jewish feast. Peter addressed Jews, not Gentiles (Acts 2.14, 22-23, 29, 30, 37, 38-39). He knew what the prophets wrote and Pentecost began the fulfillment of their prophecies. If this was the beginning of the Church, the body of Christ, Peter would have addressed Jews and Gentiles, not just Jews.
3. Peter's address said nothing about the Church, the body of Christ, in which Jew and Gentile are equal in Christ. Everything in Peter's address was Jewish; Gentiles were not in view. The idea of Jew and Gentile being equal was absent from the thinking of Peter and the rest of the apostles.
4. Peter addressed the Jews about the crime of crucifying their Messiah. When they asked him

what they should do, did Peter tell them to believe Christ died for their sins and rose from the dead for salvation (Paul's gospel)? No. He told them, "Repent and be baptized, every one of you in the name of Jesus Christ, for forgiveness of your sins and you will receive the gift of the Holy Spirit" (Acts 2.38). Is this the message of salvation today for one who becomes a member of the Church?

5. Peter told the Jews to be baptized "in the name of Jesus Christ" (Acts 2.38) and healed the lame man at the Temple "on the faith of His name" (Acts 3.16). "His name," spoke of Jesus' identity, who He was, throughout the Gospels. This was the gospel of the kingdom. Did Peter tell the lame man to believe Christ died for his sins and rose from the dead for salvation (Acts 3.6)? Did he tell the Jews this after the healing of the lame man (Acts 3.11-21)? Why not if the Church began at Pentecost? The message, the content of Paul's gospel, the gospel of salvation for those who become members of the Church, is not to believe in Christ's *identity* (cf. Matthew 16.16; John 1.49, 11.27; Acts 8.37) but to believe in His *work*—He died for our sins and rose from the dead. Peter said nothing of this at Pentecost.
6. After Pentecost, Peter continued to address only Jews (cf. Acts 3.2-26, 4.8-12). If the Church began at Pentecost, why did Peter not address Gentiles?
7. Those who believed Peter's message sold their possessions and held everything in common (Acts 2.44-45). Does the Church, the body of Christ, do this? If the Church begin at Pentecost, why not? Why do church members not hold everything in common like those who believed Peter's message after Pentecost? What would happen if a pastor told his congregation to sell everything—stocks, bonds, houses, lands, etc. and put the proceeds into a common fund for all to use?
8. If the Church began at Pentecost, what was the case of Ananias and Sapphira (Acts 5.1-11)

who sold their possessions but concealed some of the proceeds? Peter declared they lied to the Holy Spirit and God struck them dead. Is this the nature of the Church, the body of Christ today? What happened to Ananias and Sapphira was a picture of Christ's earthly kingdom where He will rule with a rod of iron. Peter exercised the authority the Lord gave the Twelve to rule and judge the twelve tribes in the kingdom (Matthew 19.28). The Lord did not promise authority over the Church, the body of Christ, but rule over Israel, Jews. How could the Church begin at Pentecost when the Lord gave them no authority over the Church?

9. What are we to make of the healings, signs and wonders that continued, the lame man Peter and John healed at the Temple (Acts 3.1-10), the apostles' healing the sick and removing demons (Acts 5.12-16), Philip's healing and expelling demons in Samaria (Acts 8.5-7)? Do these acts characterize the Church, the body of Christ? If not, why not? These miracles were signs to prove to Israel that the apostles' message that Jesus was the Christ was true.
10. If the Church began at Pentecost, why were all believers not filled with the Holy Spirit? Acts 8.14-19 states Peter and John went to Samaria after they learned the Samaritans had been saved and prayed for them to receive the Holy Spirit. Does this sound like the Church? Do fellow believers pray for new believers to receive the Holy Spirit in the Church? Over a decade after Pentecost is the account of Acts 19.2-6, Paul's encounter with believers who knew nothing of the coming of the Holy Spirit. Paul laid his hands on them and they received the Holy Spirit (Acts 19.2-6). If the Church began at Pentecost, why did these believers not have the Spirit? For the Church, the body of Christ, one who believes Paul's gospel is immediately indwelt with the Spirit (1 Corinthians 12.13; 2 Corinthians 1.22, 5.5; Ephesians 1.13). It is not a later event.

11. How was the Ethiopian eunuch saved after Philip witnessed to him? Did he believe Christ died for his sins and rose from the dead, how one becomes a member of the Church, the body of Christ? Was this what Philip told him? Acts 8 states Philip proclaimed the gospel to him—Jesus—the gospel of the kingdom—Jesus of Nazareth was the Messiah. The Ethiopian responded, "I believe Jesus Christ is the Son of the God" (Acts 8.37). Is the message of salvation today to believe Jesus is the Son of God? Or, is one saved by believing Christ died for one's sins and rose from the dead? What occurred next? The Ethiopian was baptized. Several passages state that under the gospel of the kingdom, water baptism was required for salvation (Mark 1.4, 16.16; John 3.5; Acts 2.38, 22.16). Is water baptism required for salvation under Paul's gospel? Is water baptism required to become a member of the Church, the body of Christ? Paul wrote there is *one* baptism, the baptism of the Holy Spirit (Ephesians 4.5). One means one. Water baptism is outside the realm of salvation under Paul's gospel. *No church should be practicing water baptism*. To do so is to disobey God.
12. What did Paul believe in the case of his own salvation? When he met the Lord on the road to Damascus, he asked, "Who are you, Lord?" That was the appropriate question under the gospel of the kingdom. The Lord asked His disciples, "Who do you say I am?" Peter responded that He was the Christ, the Son of the living God (Matthew 16.15-16). After Paul was saved, what did he immediately proclaim in the synagogues? He declared, "He is the Son of the God" (Acts 9.20). Paul was also water baptized for remission of sins. Ananias declared, "When you get up, be baptized and wash away your sins after you call on the name of the Lord" (Acts 22.16). Are our sins washed away with water baptism? No. We have forgiveness of sins by believing Christ died for us and rose from the dead, Paul's gospel (1 Corinthians

15.1-4; Galatians 1.11-12; Ephesians 6.19). This did not occur at Pentecost.

13. Throughout Acts, before Paul's salvation, the salvation message was proclaimed to Jews only. No Gentile evangelism occurred. Acts 8.1 (several years after Pentecost) states that even under intense persecution the apostles did not leave Jerusalem. Why? Their focus was Israel's repentance. For Jesus to return, every Jew had to repent (Acts 2.36, 38-39; cf. Matthew 23.37-39). Jesus gave them the order of their ministry: Jerusalem, Judea, Samaria, and then the ends of the earth (Acts 1.8), Jew first. Is this the order of evangelism in the Church?
14. Acts 10 records Peter's receiving the vision of the sheet and the command to go to Cornelius' house, a Gentile. If Peter and the apostles were evangelizing Gentiles, why the command? Why did Peter tell Cornelius it was not permitted for a Jew to visit and associate with a Gentile if they were evangelizing Gentiles (Acts 10.28)? Does this sound like the Church, in which Jew and Gentile are equal in Christ, with no distinction between Jew and Gentile?
15. When Cornelius and his household believed Peter's message and the Holy Spirit came on them, why were Peter and the six Jews with him astonished "that the gift of the Holy Spirit had been poured out even on the Gentiles" (Acts 10.45). If the Church began at Pentecost does this make any sense?
16. After Peter returned to Jerusalem, why did the Jewish leaders in Jerusalem upbraid him for visiting Cornelius? They declared, "You went to uncircumcised men—and ate with them!" (Acts 11.3). If the Church began at Pentecost, would Gentiles not have been brought into the Church after over a decade? If the Holy Spirit came on and had been indwelling both Jews and Gentiles at Pentecost, why did Peter say, "Therefore, if the God gave the same gift to them as also to us after we believed on the Lord Jesus Christ, how could I hinder the God (Acts 11.17)? How did they reply? They said, "So the

God gave repentance to life also to the Gentiles" (Acts 11.18). If the Church began at Pentecost, does Peter's statement make any sense? Does their response make any sense?

17. If Gentiles were being brought into the Church, the body of Christ, since Pentecost, why does Acts 11.19 state that those who were scattered as a result of Stephen's persecution (Acts 8.1, 4) travelled to Phoenicia, Cyprus, and Antioch, "speaking the word to no one except Jews only?" Could the Church begin at Pentecost if no Gentile evangelism occurred for more than a decade?
18. Why did the Twelve send Barnabas to Antioch (Acts 11.22-24) when they learned Gentiles were being saved from the Jewish ministry noted in Acts 11.20? What was the gospel they proclaimed? They proclaimed "the gospel—the Lord Jesus"—the gospel of the kingdom, who Jesus was, His identity—not that He died for our sins and rose from the dead.
19. Why was the first thing Barnabas did once he confirmed Gentiles were being saved was to go and find Paul and bring him to Antioch (Acts 11.25-26)? Were the Jerusalem leaders unable to deal with Gentile believers if the Church began more than a decade earlier?
20. How could Paul write that the Church was a secret God revealed to him, unknown in other generations, if the Church began at Pentecost (Ephesians 3.1-10, 6.19)? What occurred at Pentecost was no secret. Jeremiah and Ezekiel wrote about it 600 years before Christ. Jesus told His apostles to stay in Jerusalem until they were "clothed with power from on high" (Luke 24.49). None of this was a secret. What *was* secret was that God would create a new entity, the Church, the body of Christ, in which Jew and Gentile were equal in Christ through faith alone, believing Christ died for one's sins and rose from the dead. That did not happen at Pentecost.

If the Church did not begin at Pentecost, when did it begin? As the Scriptures are clear the Church did not begin at Pentecost, they are equally clear about when it did begin. They state the Church, the body of Christ, began with Paul.
Consider the passage:

> [10] According to the grace of the God given to me, as *a* wise master-builder, I laid *the* foundation, and another builds on *it*. But let each one who builds take heed how he builds. [11] For no one can lay another foundation besides the one which is laid, who is Jesus the Christ (1 Corinthians 3.10-11).

Some maintain these verses refer only to the local Corinthian church. Such a view cannot stand in light of Paul's language. Paul initially addressed the local Corinthian church but then spoke about the whole Church, the body of Christ. Four factors demonstrate this: 1) Paul's expression "the grace of the God given to me" identified his commission as the apostle of the Gentiles (Romans 11.13), beyond the Corinthian church; 2) Christ as the foundation spoke of the whole Church, beyond just the Corinthian church; 3) Paul declared he laid the foundation of the Church, Christ; 4) the works of wood, hay, stubble, gold, silver, precious stones judged on the Day of Christ (verses 12-15) belong to all members of the Church, not just the Corinthians. What Paul wrote the Corinthians agrees with what he wrote the Ephesians in chapter 3, that the Church was a secret before God revealed it to and through him.

Paul called himself "a wise master builder," "a wise architect," ὡς σοφὸς ἀρχιτέκτων. A contractor or architect begins a construction project. He does not enter a building operation after construction has begun. This alone tells us the Church could not have begun before Paul. A foundation is laid at the beginning and Paul wrote he laid the Church's foundation. Once cannot construct a building without a foundation and Paul wrote that the foundation is Christ. He is the foundation of the Church as He is the foundation of God's prophetic program. Christ is the foundation of all of God's programs.

Should the reader remain unconvinced, consider what Paul wrote Timothy:

> [15] The saying is trustworthy and worthy of all acceptance: Christ Jesus came into the world to save sinners: of whom I am first. [16] But because of this I was shown mercy, that in me first, Jesus Christ might demonstrate the full patience as *a* pattern for those about to believe on Him for eternal life (1 Timothy 1.15-16).

Most translations render verse 15 to read that Paul was the "worst," "chief," or "foremost" sinner rather than the "first sinner." For example, "of whom I am chief" (KJV), "and I am the worst of them" (NET), "of whom I am the worst" (NIV), "so that in me as the foremost sinner" (NASB). Paul was a great sinner, which he admitted in verse 13. But this is not the point of the passage.

The Greek text reads, Χριστὸς Ἰησοῦς ἦλθεν εἰς τὸν κόσμον ἁμαρτωλοὺς σῶσαι ὧν πρῶτός εἰμι ἐγώ, "Christ Jesus came into the world to save sinners: of whom I am first." Paul wrote he was "first," πρῶτός, not "worst." Why have translators rendered the Greek text to convey that Paul was the worst sinner? Besides being an egregiously poor translation, do they believe (or expect anyone else to believe) Paul thought he was worse than the tyrants throughout history, worse than the Caesars of his day?

Translators render the passage as they have for two reasons. First, they magnify Paul's statement in verse 13, that he was a "blasphemer, and a persecutor, and insolent," and continue this thought into verse 15. They circumvent the rest of verse 13 where he wrote he was ignorant and acted in unbelief and verse 14 where he wrote that God showed him mercy because of this. But the second, and primary reason, is that they do not understand Paul's apostleship. They do not recognize Paul was God's unique apostle, not an appendage to the Twelve, not a thirteenth apostle. Paul was the ascended Lord's previously handpicked (προχειρίζω) apostle (Acts 22.14, 26.16) to reveal a new program, the Church, the body of Christ, which He had kept secret.

How are we to understand what Paul meant when he wrote he was the "first sinner?" Clearly, Paul was not the "first sinner" in the sense of Adam. Rather, he was "first" in the sense that he was the prototype to begin a new divine program—the Church, the body of Christ. How do we know πρῶτός means "first" and not "worst?" An examination of how Paul used πρῶτός in other verses shows he always used it in its primary sense: first in time, place, etc. (Romans 10.19; 1 Corinthians 14.30, 15.3, 45, 47; Ephesians 6.2; Philippians 1.5; 1 Timothy 1.15, 2.13, 5.12; 2 Timothy 2.6, 4.16). Oher passages reveal πρῶτός has the sense of origin or originator. For example, in Revelation 1.17, the Lord says, ἐγώ εἰμι ὁ πρῶτος καὶ ὁ ἔσχατος, "I am the first and the last" (cf. Revelation 1.11, 22.13).

Verse 16 cements Paul's meaning. He wrote "in me first," ἐν ἐμοὶ πρώτῳ.[6] Paul's being "first" meant he was God's archetype, God's prototype. Verse 16 reveals Paul's salvation was a "pattern," ὑποτύπωσιν, for all who would be saved afterward through his gospel (1 Corinthians 15.1-4). A pattern is made first as a model or standard for what will follow. God displayed His "full patience," the extent of His mercy in Paul. Paul was God's apostle of grace for God displayed His marvelous grace in saving Paul and giving him the gospel that Christ died for our sins, rose from the dead for our justification, and that by simply believing this one can have forgiveness of sins and eternal life. Salvation has never been easier.

---

[6] The KJV translators corrected their error in verse 15 and rendered the phrase correctly, "in me first" (KJV). Other translators compound their error: "in me as the worst" (NET), "the worst of sinners" (NIV), "as the foremost sinner" (NASB).

Those who teach the Church began at Pentecost commit two flagrant theological errors. The first is the failure to understand God's covenant program with Israel. As a result, it is conflated and confused with God's program of the Church. The second is the failure to understand that the Church is a *new creation*, which God had kept hidden. Pentecost began nothing new. It fulfilled God's promise to Israel, which He made hundreds of years before.

The consequence of the great error of teaching the Church began at Pentecost is massive confusion and misunderstanding regarding Church theology. Indeed, those who teach the Church began at Pentecost *do not and cannot understand Church theology*. If the foundation is unsound, can the structure be sound?

A final point will be repeated. Throughout the Gospels and early Acts, the gospel of salvation was based on Jesus' *identity*, believing who He was—the Christ, the Son of God. This is clear in the Gospels from the salvation accounts in Matthew 16.16; John 1.49, 11.27; Acts 8.37. John summed this truth as he concluded his gospel. He wrote:

> [30] Therefore, Jesus did many other signs also in the presence of His disciples that are not written in this book. [31] But these have been written so you may believe that Jesus is the Christ, the Son of the God, and that believing, you may have life in His name (John 20.30-31).

What was the message of salvation proclaimed by John the Baptist, Jesus, the Twelve? It was to believe Jesus was the Christ, the Son of God.

The salvation message for members of the Church is to believe in Christ's *work*—His death and resurrection. Such a distinction is shown in *type* in the story of Jonah. God told Jonah to go to Nineveh—to Gentiles. Jonah disobeyed, boarded a ship, and sailed the opposite direction. God caused a storm and Jonah was thrown into the sea where a great sea creature swallowed him. He was in the belly of the beast three days and three nights until the whale expelled him onto land. His experience pictured Christ's death and resurrection (Matthew 12.40). Jonah then went to Nineveh—to minister to Gentiles.

What is the point? Only after Jonah experienced a type of death and resurrection did he go to Nineveh—to Gentiles. Jonah's experience was in *type*, Paul's gospel. Only after Jesus died and rose from the dead did the Lord reveal the message of salvation for Gentiles (primarily) was based on His death, burial, and resurrection (1 Corinthians 15.1-4).

Peter and the other apostles did not proclaim Christ's death and resurrection for salvation until *after* the Council of Jerusalem in 51 A.D. Peter concluded that Jews must from then on be saved like Paul's Gentiles, by Paul's gospel (Acts 15.1-11). Before this, they had proclaimed the gospel of the kingdom, Christ's identity. After the Lord saved Paul, however, the Lord revealed the significance of His death and resurrection for salvation (Galatians 1.11-12). Paul became the apostle of the Gentiles (Romans 11.13) even as Jonah became the messenger to Gentiles in Nineveh after his typical death and resurrection.

The Scriptures are clear: God began the Church with Paul and revealed all Church doctrine to Paul and through Paul. Thus, all Church theology is found in Paul's thirteen letters, Romans through Philemon. Apart from this recognition, understanding Church theology is impossible.

As God's apostle through whom the ascended Lord founded the Church, the body of Christ, the Thessalonians became imitators of Paul and of the Lord "for you received the word in much affliction, with *the* joy of *the* Holy Spirit, so you became *an* example to all the believers in Macedonia and Achaia (verses 6-7).

The Thessalonian's receiving the word "in much affliction," ἐν θλίψει πολλῇ, resulted from unbelieving

Jews who formed a mob, incited a riot, and attacked Jason's house where Paul and his companions were staying (Acts 17.5-9). Despite these dangers and threats, they received the word of God "with joy of the Holy Spirit," μετὰ χαρᾶς πνεύματος ἁγίου. The account of their faith and courage spread to all believers in Macedonia and Achaia (verse 7), northern and southern Greece, respectively. In addition, Paul wrote that the Lord's word had gone forth from them even beyond Greece "in every place," ἐν παντὶ τόπῳ (verse 8). Thus, Paul wrote, "Your faith toward the God has gone abroad so that we do not have to say anything." What a testimony!

Comparing Luke's record in Acts and Paul's words to the Thessalonians provides an interesting contrast. After Thessalonica, Paul and Silas went to the synagogue of the Jews in Berea. Luke wrote,

> 11 Now these were more noble than those in Thessalonica. They received the word with all eagerness, by examining the Scriptures every day, if these things were so.
> 12 Therefore, many of them believed, along with quite a few of the prominent Greek women and men (Acts 17.11-12).

Luke wrote that the Bereans eagerly received the word and were "more noble" than those in Thessalonica. But nothing more of these believers is known after this. They disappear. In contrast, Paul wrote two letters to the Thessalonians and sent Timothy to encourage them in their persecution. While Luke declared that the Bereans were "more noble," it was the testimony of the Thessalonians that became widespread and they were an example to all believers in Macedonia, Achaia, and every other place (verse 8). Everyone knew of their faith. Paul wrote, "For they themselves report about how you welcomed us and how you turned to the God from the idols to serve *the* living and true God and to wait for His Son from the heavens, whom He raised from the dead, Jesus, the One who will rescue us from the coming wrath" (verse 9). What is the lesson? Perseverance.

It is wonderful to receive the word of God eagerly and examine the Scriptures. But the Christian life is not a sprint but a long-distance race. Readily receiving God's word is commendable. More laudable is continuing in it for it is how we grow in Christ and live lives pleasing to Him. Such living demonstrates we are different and proclaims God's grace and power.
The Gentile world was rife with idols and worship of false gods. When Paul visited Athens, one of the great intellectual centers of the ancient world, he was appalled by the profusion of idols (Acts 17.16-34). Petronius, the Roman courtier and writer who was a contemporary of Paul, satirically quipped about Athens through Quartilla, "Our region is so full of deities that you may more frequently meet with a god than a man."[7] Such reality reveals that intellectuals are often as deceived and unenlightened as those less well-educated. Cicero expressed then when he wrote, "Somehow or other no statement is too absurd for some philosophers to make."[8]

The Thessalonians turned to God from idolatry (verse 9). While few have physical idols in the modern world, idolatry is as prevalent today as it was in Paul's day. Our idolatry is materialism—the view that all that exists is the material world. The word "idolatry," εἰδωλολατρεία, comes from the verb εἴδω, "see" and the noun λατρεία, "service." It means serving what is seen, the creation, rather than the Creator. Evolution is our expression of idolatry. If Petronius lived today, he would write the same as he did two millennia ago.

Those in the ancient world knew an idol was not a god but a representation of a god. Today, mankind worships the natural world as if were God.[9] Paul wrote the Romans:

> 22 While they profess to be wise, they became fools 23 and changed the glory of the immortal God into *a* likeness of *an*

---

7 Petronius Arbiter. *Satyricon*. Sec. 17.
8 Cicero. *De Divinatione*, 2.58.119
9 In the Tribulation, most of humanity will worship images of the Beast.

> image of mortal man, and birds, and quadrupeds, and reptiles. [24] Therefore, the God gave them up to the desires of their hearts to uncleanness—to dishonor their bodies among themselves. [25] They exchanged the truth of the God into the lie and worshiped and served the creation rather than the Creator, who is blessed forever. Amen (Romans 1.22-25).

Despite pervasive paganism, the Thessalonians responded to Paul's preaching. They turned from their idols to the living God. They believed his message of salvation and experienced "*the* power of God for salvation to everyone who believes" (Romans 1.16).

A similar thing occurred in Ephesus. Luke recorded that as a result of Paul's preaching, the Ephesians burned their sorcery books (Acts 19.19) and threw away their idols (Acts 19.23-41). When people believe the gospel, they leave the kingdom of darkness and enter the kingdom of light. Behavior changes. In today's world, those who come to know the living God abandon materialism and evolution, modern paganism and idolatry, even as the idolaters of Paul's day. Nothing is greater or more powerful than God's gospel of grace. It is the message of life, the sole hope for victory over sin and death.

As the Thessalonians learned from Paul's teaching about the Rapture, expounded in chapter 4, they waited for Christ, God's Son "whom He raised from the dead" (verse 10). Notice Paul's gospel.

To what end did they wait for Christ? They waited for Him to rescue them from the coming wrath, the Tribulation. This is as clear a statement of the Pre-Tribulational Rapture as can be made.

"To wait for His Son from the heavens" is the Rapture and "the coming wrath" is the Tribulation, Daniel's 70th week (verse 10). As will be seen, the Lord comes from heaven to meet members of His Church in the sky. Paul used the noun "wrath," ὀργή, twice more in this letter (1 Thessalonians 2.16, 5.9). The latter verse fortified what he wrote in verse 10.

When Paul used ὀργή, "wrath," with God as the subject, he meant the Tribulation, the Day of the Lord, which according to Daniel 9.27 lasts seven years. He expected the Rapture to occur in his lifetime after which the Tribulation would come, ending in Christ's Second Advent. The Scriptures reveal all the apostles expected end-time events to occur soon (cf. Matthew 3.1-2, 4.17, 10.5-7, 16.28, 24.32-35, 26.62-64; John 21.22-23; Acts 2.14-21, 3.19-21; Hebrews 10.24-25, 36-37; James 5-7-8; 1 Peter 1.3-6, 4.7; 1 John 2.18; Jude 1.17-18; Revelation 1.1-3, 22.6-7, 22.10-12).

In Paul's sentence, "the One who rescues us from the coming wrath," τὸν ῥυόμενον ἡμᾶς ἀπὸ τῆς ὀργῆς τῆς ἐρχομένης, both participles of the verbs ῥύομαι and ἔρχομαι are presents, but have a future sense. Christ rescues members of the Church, the body of Christ, from God's future, coming wrath. In the prepositional phrase, "from the coming wrath," Paul used the preposition ἀπό, rather than ἐκ. Thus, the Son comes "from the heavens," ἐκ τῶν οὐρανῶν, "out of" the heavens, and after He comes, He will rescue His Church, "from the coming wrath," ἀπὸ τῆς ὀργῆς τῆς ἐρχομένης. The prepositions ἐκ and ἀπό are distinct in terms of "separation." The former has the sense "out of" while the latter has the sense, "away from." Christ rescues His Church "away from" wrath, the Tribulation. Had Paul used ἐκ "out of," one might argue believers could experience *some* of the Tribulation and then Christ would take them "out of" it. But ἀπό removes this possibility. The Lord will withdraw His Church "away from" any contact with God's wrath. Paul wrote in chapter 4, that members of the Church, the body of Christ, whether dead or alive, meet Him in the air and go "away from" the coming wrath.

Verse 10 proves the Pre-Tribulational Rapture. Instead of accepting it, those who reject the Pre-Tribulation Rapture compound their error by rejecting the rest of the Scriptures that teach it for it does not fit their theology. The evidence for the Pre-Tribulation Rapture is overwhelming but its opponents will not believe it because they do not *want* to believe it.

Excursus: When Will the Rapture Occur?

Before proceeding further, the question of when the Rapture occurs should be addressed. Five major views are taught. One is correct. They are the following:

1. Post-Tribulation: Believers are raptured at the end of Tribulation, when Christ returns in judgment.
2. Pre-Wrath: Believers are raptured somewhere between the sixth and seventh seals in Revelation 6.
3. Mid-Tribulation: Believers are raptured at the middle of the Tribulation.
4. Partial Rapture: Only faithful believers are raptured at the beginning of the Tribulation.
5. Pre-Tribulation: Believers are raptured before the Tribulation.

The first three views have the Church present in the Tribulation, in Daniel's 70th week. These views are easily dismissed as false for the Tribulation concerns prophecy and the Church has no prophecy associated with it. The great error of these three views is failure to distinguish God's program for Israel and the nations and God's program for the Church. In essence, they do not understand what the Church is. They do not understand the Church is a new creation God revealed to Paul. Paul wrote the Ephesians that the Church was unknown in previous generations, not made known to mankind (Ephesians 3.1-7). He wrote that "the dispensation of the grace of the God" (Ephesians 3.2) began the Church and that this dispensation was a secret the ascended Christ gave to Paul to reveal (Ephesians 3.2-3). He described this as "the secret of the Christ" (Ephesians 3.4). God's prophetic plan for Israel and the nations (Gentiles) was no secret. Thousands of verses in the Old Testament reveal this plan. Jesus spoke of it extensively in His earthly ministry. What was secret, however, was that God would create a new plan, a new creation, the Church, in which Jew and Gentile were equal in Christ, identified in His death and resurrection, indwelt by the Holy Spirit, saved by Paul's gospel, that Christ died for one's sins and rose from the dead, and that this salvation was by faith alone. The Old Testament and Gospels revealed none of this. Failure by theologians to recognize this central truth has led not only to error regarding the Rapture but error in understanding Church theology.

As the three views above, the fourth view, that only faithful believers are raptured, it is easily dismissed by the Scriptures. Paul wrote in 1 Thessalonians 4.14 the criterion for being in the Rapture. It is "if we believe that Jesus died and rose." In 1 Corinthians 15.51, he wrote that "we will all be changed," every member of the Church, the body of Christ, faithful or unfaithful.

Having shown the first four views are false, one is left: the Pre-Tribulation Rapture. The Scriptures are exceedingly clear that God will complete and resurrect members of the Church, the body of Christ, who have died and transform members of the Church who are alive, before He initiates His prophetic program with Israel and the nations. Not a word about the Church is present in the Old Testament, Gospels, or book of Revelation.

Errors about the timing of the Rapture result from failing to understand that that the Church is a new creation the risen Christ revealed to Paul, that the Church was a secret, and that it is outside prophecy. If one will keep God's revelation about His programs for Israel and the nations separate from His program for the Church, one will have sound theology. If one will not, confusion and false teaching is the result. Sadly, most of Christendom has failed to understand these simple truths and this failure accounts for the great confusion and division that exists.

1 Thessalonians 2

Encouragement of the Thessalonians

1 For yourselves know, brethren, that our coming to you has not been for nothing.
2 But although we suffered and were mistreated, as you know, in Philippi, we were bold in our God to declare God's gospel to you amid much opposition.
3 For our appeal *is* not from deceit, or from impurity, or from trickery.
4 But, as we have been approved by the God to be entrusted with the gospel, so we speak, not to please men, but the God who examines our hearts.
5 For at no time did we use flattering speech, as you know, or pretense for greed—God *is* witness!—
6 or seek praise from men, neither from you or from others, though as Christ's apostles, we have weighty authority.
7 Rather, we were gentle[1] among you, as *a* nurse would cherish her own children.
8 So, as we yearned over you, we kept being pleased, not only because we shared the gospel of the God to you, but also our own lives, because you became dear to us.
9 For you remember brethren, our labor and toil: by working night and day so we might not burden any of you, we declared the gospel of the God to you.
10 You *are* witnesses—and the God—how holily, and righteously, and blamelessly we were to you who believe.
11 Just as each one of you know, as *a* father his own children, we exhorted, and encouraged, and implored you
12 to walk worthily of the God, who calls you into His own kingdom and glory.

Comment:

Verses 1-13: Paul reminded the Thessalonians how their (Paul, Silas, Timothy) coming was not in vain (verse 1). Despite the abuse they endured in Philippi,

---

[1] Some manuscripts read ἤπιοι, "gentle," and others read νήπιοι, "little children."

"we were bold in our God," ἐπαρρησιασάμεθα ἐν τῷ θεῷ ἡμῶν (verse 2). As noted above, Paul's boldness came from relying on God, the power of His word and the Spirit (cf. 1 Thessalonians 1.5). Without God's word and His Spirit, we are powerless to change lives for eternity. God alone can do this. As Christians, our job is to speak truth, to proclaim the gospel and the Scriptures as clearly as possible and let God work.

Luke recorded the abuse Paul and Silas suffered at Philippi. While there, Paul freed a girl possessed with a "spirit of Python" from her demon. In Greek mythology, Python was the snake or dragon that guarded the oracle of Delphi people consulted to learn the future. As a result of Paul's expelling the girl's demon, thereby removing her masters' source of divination, they had Paul and Silas arrested and the authorities severely beat and imprisoned them.

Throughout his ministry, Paul worked in a climate of opposition. Believers in Christ operate in enemy territory—behind enemy lines, opposed by Satan, the god of this age (2 Corinthians 4.4; cf. Matthew 4.8-9) who has created a theater of deceit to blind humanity to reality and confuse God's word. The gospel and the Scriptures are God's counter-narrative.

Paul wrote, "our appeal is not from deceit, or from impurity, or from trickery" (verse 3). Paul wrote this was because his opponents claimed he was a deceiver. Nothing has changed. Many still attack Paul, claiming he perverted Jesus' teachings and that he was a false teacher. Those who make these attacks are enemies of Christ, though they may claim to be Christians. How can they be believers when they attack Paul, who proclaimed the gospel by which we are saved—Christ died for our sins and rose from the dead?

In verse 4, Paul declared, "we have been approved by the God to be entrusted with the gospel." The risen, glorified Lord "previously handpicked," προχειρίζω (cf. Acts 22.14, 26.16) Paul as His apostle to the Gentiles to reveal His gospel of grace. On this basis, Paul declared "we have been approved by the God," δεδοκιμάσμεθα ὑπὸ τοῦ θεοῦ. The verb "approved," δοκιμάζω, was used to test or determine if something was genuine, e.g., metals. God approved and certified Paul and his ministry.

Paul continued in verse 4, "so we speak, not to please men, but the God, who examines our hearts." Paul pursued pleasing God, not men. He forsook all he had had as a rising Pharisee after he came to know the risen Christ on the road to Damascus. He wrote the Galatians:

> [13] For you heard of my former way of life in the Judaism, that beyond measure I used to persecute the congregation of the God, and used to destroy it. [14] And I kept advancing in Judaism above many contemporaries among my race, since I was intensely zealous for the traditions of my fathers. [15] But when it pleased the God, who set me apart from my mother's womb and called *me* through His grace [16] to reveal His Son in me so I might proclaim Him among the Gentiles, I immediately consulted not with flesh and blood, [17] or went up to Jerusalem to the apostles before me, but I went into Arabia and returned again to Damascus (Galatians 1.13-17).

To the Philippians, he wrote:

> [7] But whatever things were gain to me, I have regarded them loss, because of the Christ. [8] But doubtless, I regard all things to be loss because of the superiority of the knowledge of Christ Jesus my Lord, for whom I lost all the things and regard them as dung, so I might gain Christ, [9] and might be found in Him—not having my righteousness, which *is* from Law, but the righteousness from God which *is* through *the* faithfulness of Christ, by the faith (Philippians 3.7-9).

Paul served the risen Christ and relied on His power. He is our model. Like Paul, we should seek to please God, not men.

Paul never used "flattering speech," λόγῳ κολακείας or "pretense for greed," προφάσει πλεονεξίας in his ministry (verse 5). He continued, stating that he did not "seek praise from men, neither from you or from others, though as Christ's apostles, we have weighty authority" (verse 6).

Once Christ's greatest enemy, Paul faced intense opposition after the Lord saved him. He wrote the Corinthians about false teachers, whom he mockingly called "super apostles," λίαν ἀποστόλων, likely how they promoted themselves (2 Corinthians 11.5-7, 12.11-13). Paul's authority was from the high command, the Lord Himself. When forced to defend his apostleship according to "human standards," Paul noted his qualifications to the Corinthians:

> [16] Again I say, no one should think me to be *a* fool. But even if you do, receive me as *a* fool, so I might boast *a* little. [17] What I say, I do not say according to *the* Lord, but as in foolishness, in this boastful confidence. [18] Since many boast according to human standards, I will boast too—[19] for you gladly entertain the fools—since you are so smart. [20] For you permit it if anyone enslaves you, if anyone exploits *you*, if anyone takes advantage of you, if anyone exalts himself, if anyone slaps your face. [21] To my shame, I say, We have been weak! But in whatever anyone may dare—in foolishness I say *it*—I dare too! [22] Are they Hebrews? I too! Are they Israelites? I too! Are they descendants Abraham? I too! [23] Are they ministers of Christ? (I speak as unhinged), I more. Exceeding in labors, exceeding in imprisonments, in stripes beyond measure, in deaths many times. [24] Five times I received from *the* Jews forty lashes minus one. [25] Three times I was

> beaten with rods, once was I stoned, three times I was I shipwrecked. I spent *a* night and *a* day in the deep. [26] In many journeys, in dangers of rivers, in dangers of robbers, in dangers from *my* people, in dangers from Gentiles, in dangers in *the* city, in dangers in *the* wilderness, in dangers on *the* sea, in dangers among false brethren, [27] in labor and toil, in many sleepless nights, in hunger and thirst, many times without food, in cold and without clothing. [28] Besides these external things *is* the daily stress on me, the concern for all the churches. [29] Who is weak, and I am not weak? Who is offended, and I do not burn? [30] If I must boast, I will boast in the things of my weakness. [31] The God and Father of our Lord Jesus Christ knows, the One who is blessed forever, I do not lie (2 Corinthians 11.16-31)!

Dripping with sarcasm, Paul wrote to awaken the Corinthians. They had accepted those who called themselves "super apostles" but Paul exposed them as exploiters and deceivers. Paul's behavior was a complete contrast: he came with humility, supplied his own needs, taught them the truth, and loved them.

Paul's authority was "weighty" (verse 6) for it came from the ascended Lord. But he did not exercise it in an overbearing manner as the false teachers their presumed authority. Instead, he wrote, "we were gentle among you, as a nurse would cherish her own children" (verse 7). Thus, "we yearned over you, we kept being pleased, not only because we shared the gospel of the God to you, but also our own lives, because you became dear to us" (verse 8).

As the apostle of the Gentiles, the apostle of the grace of God, and the apostle of secrets,[2] the Lord gave Paul great authority. But he used it sparingly, exercising it only when necessary to instruct or correct. Paul not only declared the gospel to the Thessalonians but loved them and became close to them. He also worked

---

[2] See the author's *Paul: Apostle of Secrets.*

to support his ministry so as not to be a financial burden (verse 9). While Paul accepted donations, he did not demand payment—in contrast to the false teachers (2 Corinthians 11.5-9, 12.11-13).

Paul reminded them they were witnesses with God "how holily, and righteously, and blamelessly we were to you who believe" (verse 10). Imitating Paul, we should demonstrate such character to fellow believers.

In verses 11-12, Paul wrote, "just as each one of you know, as *a* father his own children, we exhorted, and encouraged, and implored you to walk worthily of the God, who calls you into His own kingdom and glory."

The destiny for all who put their trust in the God of the Bible is God's kingdom. For those who are part of God's prophetic program (Israel and the nations), God's kingdom is Christ's earthly kingdom. For members of the Church, God's kingdom is heaven for that is where we have citizenship (Ephesians 1.3; Philippians 3.20). Overall, God's kingdom is the realm over which He rules: Israel and the nations (Gentiles), the Church, and the holy angels (Romans 14.17; 1 Corinthians 4.20, 6.9-10, 15.24, 50; Galatians 5.21; Ephesians 5.5; Colossians 4.11; 2 Thessalonians 1.5; 2 Timothy 4.1). This is what Paul usually means when he uses the phrase.

Given this reality, Paul exhorted believers to "walk worthily" of it. Remembering *who* we are and *whose* we are should direct our behavior.

---

13 And because of this, we also continually thank the God, that when you received *the* word of the God when you heard *it* from us, you accepted it, not *as the* word of men, but as it truly is, *the* word of God, which also works in you who believe.
14 For you became imitators, brethren, of the congregations of the God that are in Judea in Christ Jesus. For you also suffered the same things as they from your own countrymen, even as they from the Jews,

15 who killed both the Lord Jesus, and the prophets, and persecuted us and do not please God and oppose all men
16 by hindering us to speak to the Gentiles so they might be saved. So they always fill up their sins. Now the wrath came on them for the end.

Comment:

Verses 13-16: With these things in mind, Paul wrote, "we also continually thank the God, that when you received *the* word of the God when you heard *it* from us, you accepted it, not *as the* word of men, but as it truly is, *the* word of God, which also works in you who believe" (verse 13). Paul taught unceasing prayer and thanksgiving throughout his letters (1 Thessalonians 1.2, 2.13, 5.17-18; Romans 1.9-10; 1 Corinthians 1.4; Ephesians 5.20, 6.18; Philippians 1.4; Colossians 1.3; 2 Thessalonians 1.3, 11; Philemon 1.4). Do you wish to have joy? Thanksgiving is the secret to joy. A thankful believer is a joyful Christian.

The Thessalonians had received Paul's gospel and it was working (ἐνεργέω) in them (verse 13). How does God's word "work" in a believer? Paul wrote that the word of God is alive and effective (Hebrews 4.12). When one believes the gospel, one receives eternal life and God begins His divine work to conform us into the image of His Son, συμμόρφους τῆς εἰκόνος τοῦ υἱοῦ αὐτοῦ. God transforms us as we believe Him and His word (Romans 8.29; 2 Corinthians 3.18; Ephesians 3.20; Philippians 2.13; Colossians 1.29), the process known as sanctification.

The word of God brings salvation. The Thessalonians heard God's word from Paul and received it. Hearing God's word produces faith. Paul described this process to the Romans:

> 13 For all who would call upon the name of *the* Lord will be saved. 14 How then could they call on *Him* whom they did not believe? But how could they believe of whom they did not hear? And how could

> they hear apart from one who preaches?
> [15] And how could they preach if they should not be sent? Just as it has been written: How beautiful *are* the feet of those who proclaim peace, of those who proclaim the good things! [16] But not all heeded the gospel. For Isaiah says: Lord, who believed our report?
> [17] So, the faith *is* from hearing but the hearing *is* through *the* word of God (Romans 10.13-17).

Peter wrote similarly:

> Because you were reborn, not from perishable seed, but imperishable, through *the* living and abiding word of God forever (1 Peter 1.23).

Some have taught God "imparts" or "injects" faith into the hearts of those He wishes to save, causing them to believe. Such an idea has no Scriptural basis. The Scriptures state that receiving God's word brings salvation. James exhorted his readers:

> Therefore, by putting away all filthiness and overflowing evil, accept with humility the implanted word that can save your souls (James 1.21).

In the case of Lydia, in Acts 16, the Scripture testifies that as she listened, the Lord opened her heart to heed the things spoken by Paul (Acts 16.14). God opens the heart but it is the word that produces faith, not God imparting or injecting faith. God wants all to be saved (1 Timothy 2.4) and does everything possible to this end without violating one's will. As will be examined in 2 Thessalonians, Paul wrote about those who perish in the Tribulation: "and by every deceit of the unrighteousness to those who perish, because they did not accept the love of the truth so they might be saved" (2 Thessalonians 2.10). They perish, not though any fault of God but because they do not accept the love of the truth so they might be saved.

Some use Ephesians 2.8-9 as a basis to claim God imparts or infuses faith so one can believe. It reads:

> [8] For by the grace you have been saved through the faith[3] and this is not from yourselves: *it is* the gift of God, [9] not from works, so no one might boast.

According to some, "the faith" or "the grace" is "the gift." Such an interpretation errs grammatically and theologically. Grammatically, a pronoun agrees with its antecedent in gender and number. If Paul meant "the grace" or "the faith" as the antecedent of "the gift," he would have used the feminine demonstrative "this" (αὕτη) rather than the neuter (τοῦτο) for "grace" and "faith" are feminine nouns. However, a *neuter* pronoun can refer to a phrase or summarize a thought. Such is the case here. The entire salvation package is "the gift of God." It is the result of God's grace through "the faith," Paul's gospel (cf. Romans 5.15-18, 6.23; 2 Corinthians 9.15; Ephesians 3.7, 4.7). Again, faith is produced by the word of God. Theologically, we have seen that salvation comes through the word of God, "the faith," Paul's gospel, which comes by God's grace.

As noted above, the Thessalonians received God's word amid much affliction and became imitators (μιμηταὶ) of Paul (1 Thessalonians 1.6). In verse 14, he declared they became imitators (μιμηταὶ) "of the congregations of the God that are in Judea in Christ Jesus," Jews who had believed the gospel of the kingdom and had come to know Christ. Both had Christ in common as well as affliction.

Paul usually used the expression "in Christ" for members of the Church, the body of Christ. But the phrase "in Christ" is a broader identification than just members of the Church. "In Christ" is equal to being a "saint," a term for all who have trusted in the God of the Bible. Consider the following passages:

---

[3] Some manuscripts do not have the definite article with faith. But the definite article is the more likely reading for most of the time when Paul did not include the definite article, διὰ πίστεως, "through faith," he used it in the expression "through faithfulness of Christ." When he included the definite article, διὰ τῆς πίστεως, he meant what was believed, his gospel and doctrines.

> Greet Andronicus and Junia, my kinsmen and my fellow prisoners, who are notable among the apostles, who also were before me in Christ (Romans 16.7).

> Now I was not known by face to the Judean congregations that *are* in Christ (Galatians 1.22).

> [15] But sanctify the Lord God in your hearts, always ready to give *an* answer to everyone who asks you for *an* account about the hope that *is* in you—yet with gentleness and respect, [16] by having *a* good conscience, so the ones who revile your good conduct in Christ might be ashamed when they speak against you (1 Peter 3.15-16).

> Greet one another with a kiss of love. Peace *be* to you all who *are* in Christ Jesus! Amen (1 Peter 5.14).

The Thessalonians suffered from their own countrymen as believing Jews had suffered from their own countrymen, Jews who rejected Christ (verse 14).

In verses 15-16, Paul wrote that the Jews who persecuted believing Jews were those, "who killed both the Lord Jesus, and the prophets, and persecuted us and do not please God and oppose all men by hindering us to speak to the Gentiles so they might be saved. So they always fill up their sins. Now the wrath came on them for the end."

The enemies of God exist in every generation. Israel's history is replete with examples of those who opposed God and killed His prophets. In the accounts of Kings and Chronicles, most of Judah's kings were evil, and all of Israel's kings were evil. Most rulers and the vast majority of humanity oppose Christ. In Paul's ministry, unbelieving Jews persecuted him and tried to kill him. He wrote that such actions "do not please God and oppose all men" (verse 15).

According to God's prophetic plan, Christ cannot return to establish His kingdom on earth until Israel repents (Matthew 23.37-39). While many thousands of Jews repented and believed in Christ, the vast majority did not.

On Cyprus, during his first missionary journey, Paul encountered a Jewish false prophet named Bar-Jesus, also known as Elymas.[4] Bar-Jesus means "son of Jesus," "son of Joshua." He became a sorcerer, a μάγος, (Acts 13.6), but not like the Magi, μάγοι, who worshipped the newborn Jesus. The Magi were godly believers, while Elymas was a false prophet (Acts 13.6). Paul called him a "son of *the* Devil," υἱὲ διαβόλου (Acts 13.10), what Jesus called the Jews in John 8.44. Elymas tried to prevent his employer, the Roman proconsul Sergius Paulus, from hearing the gospel. As a result of this opposition, the Lord blinded him after Paul declared he would be blind for a season (Acts 13.11). Elymas' blindness was a picture of Israel's national, spiritual blindness until the nation repents and Christ comes (Romans 11.25). At the end of the Tribulation, when all hope appears lost, God will save the entire Jewish nation that remains alive in the Tribulation (Romans 11.26; Isaiah 66.8). Every Jew will repent and believe Jesus of Nazareth is the Messiah. This will fulfill the condition Jesus made when He declared:

> 37 Jerusalem, Jerusalem, the one who kills the prophets and stones the ones who have been sent to her! How often I wished to gather your children, as *a* hen gathers her chicks under her wings, and you would not! 38 Behold, your house is left to you desolate! 39 For I tell you, you should never see Me from now until you should say, Blessed *is* the One who comes in *the* name of *the* Lord (Matthew 23.37-39).

Despite Elymas' attempt to prevent Sergius Paulus from hearing God's word, he became a believer when he saw what happened to Elymas—"he was astonished

[4] The etymology and meaning of "Elymas" has been discussed at length with no reliable conclusion.

at the doctrine of the Lord" (Acts 13.12). Sergius Paulus heard and was saved through Paul's message.

God loves mankind. He wants all to be saved, to be free from sin and death and have eternal life. Those who oppose God and the message of salvation "always fill up their sins," ἀναπληρῶσαι αὐτῶν τὰς ἁμαρτίας πάντοτε. Thus, "the wrath came on them for the end," ἔφθασεν δὲ ἐπ' αὐτοὺς ἡ ὀργὴ εἰς τέλος (verse 16). The aorist "came on," ἔφθασεν, is proleptic, i.e., "will come." The expression, "the wrath," ἡ ὀργὴ, is the same wrath of 1 Thessalonians 1.10, the Tribulation, the Day of the Lord.

Paul's Longing to Visit

17 Now brethren, since we have been separated from you for the space of *an* hour, in presence, not in affection, we were exceedingly eager, greatly desiring to see your face.
18 Therefore we wanted to come to you, I, Paul, again and again, and Satan thwarted us.
19 For who *is* our hope, or joy, or crown of rejoicing? *Are* you not *it* before our Lord Jesus Christ at His coming?
20 For you are our glory and joy!

Comment:

Verses 17-20: These verses show Paul's love for the Thessalonians. While only separated "for the space of an hour," ἀφ' ὑμῶν πρὸς καιρὸν ὥρας, an idiom for a short time, he missed them dearly and longed to see them (verse 17) after he and Silas were forced to flee from Thessalonica to Berea due to Jewish persecution.

Paul wrote "again and again," καὶ ἅπαξ καὶ δίς, literally, "once and twice," he wished to see them but Satan prevented him (verse 18). Paul's words reveal the spiritual warfare waged against believers by the powers of darkness (cf. Ephesians 6.10-17). Satanic forces try to hinder and confuse God's message of salvation. Paul also wrote the Romans that many times he planned to come see them but was hindered

(Romans 1.11-13). Despite Satan's power, God is in control and will save all who will trust Him.

In verse 19, Paul rhetorically asked the Thessalonians who was his hope, joy, and crown of rejoicing (verse 19). He answered the question in verse 20: they were. Those who come to know the Lord from our testimony and grow in the Lord from our teaching are our joy and reward. What a reward! Nothing is more precious than one saved from sin and death to spend eternity with the Lord. Empires and civilizations perish. Humans are forever.

All believers belong to the Lord and we are His inheritance (Ephesians 1.18; Hebrews 2.10, 13; Psalm 2.8). Members of the Church share in this inheritance as joint heirs of Christ (Romans 8.17). Those to whom we have faithfully ministered are part of our glory that will be revealed when Christ returns.

With regard to Paul's phrase, "before our Lord Jesus Christ at His coming" in verse 19, two words should be examined: ἔμπροσθεν, "before" and παρουσία, "coming." The adverb ἔμπροσθεν is formed by two prepositions ἐν and πρός and means "before," "in the presence of," "in the sight of." The noun παρουσία is formed by the preposition παρά (to be alongside) and the verb εἰμί, "to be" and means "presence" or "coming."

Two verses in the New Testament have both words: 1 Thessalonians 2.19 and 1 Thessalonians 3.13. The adverb ἔμπροσθεν by itself is found in 2 Corinthians 5.10, 1 Thessalonians 1.3, 2.19, 3.9, 13 and used for being in Christ's presence. Paul used παρουσία in 1 Corinthians 15.23, 1 Thessalonians 2.19, 3.13, 4.15, 5.23; 2 Thessalonians 2.1, 8 for both Christ's return at His Second Advent and for the Pre-Tribulation Rapture. Context governs what "coming" Paul meant.

Thus, 1 Corinthians 15.23, 1 Thessalonians 4.15, 5.23, and 2 Thessalonians 2.1 refer to Christ's Pre-Tribulation Rapture while 2 Thessalonians 2.8 refers to His return at the Second Advent. In the context of this passage, ἔμπροσθεν and παρουσία probably refer to the Rapture than the Second Advent due to Paul's words that the Thessalonians were his "hope, or joy, or crown of rejoicing" (verse 19) and "you are our glory and joy" (verse 20). Paul's glory and joy were associated with those who believed his gospel, who became members of the Church, the body of Christ. The Rapture is part of "the day of Christ," when Christ will examine our works and give rewards to members of the Church (1 Corinthians 1.8, 3.12-15, 5.5; 2 Corinthians 1.14; Philippians 1.6, 10, 2.16; 2 Timothy 1.18, 4.8).

Christ's return in 1 Thessalonians 3.13 is His Second Advent. This verse has the words ἔμπροσθεν and παρουσία and His return is described as "with all His saints." All believers are not present at the Rapture, only members of the Church, the body of Christ. Thus, this return must be Christ's Second Advent and includes all of God's saints, everyone saved in all of God's programs along with all Christ's righteous angels (Matthew 25.31).

1 Thessalonians 3

Timothy's Visit

1 Therefore when we could stand it no longer, we
thought it best to be left alone in Athens
2 and sent Timothy, our brother and coworker of the
God in the gospel of the Christ, so he might strengthen
and encourage you about your faith,
3 so no one would be shaken by these afflictions. For
you yourselves know that we are appointed for this.
4 For even while we were with you, we kept telling you
beforehand that we were about to suffer affliction, just
as also you know happened.
5 Because of this, when I could stand it no longer, I sent
so I might know about your faith, lest somehow the
one who is tempting you somehow tempted you and
our labor would be for nothing.

Comment:

Verses 1-5: Frustrated by Satan's preventing him from seeing the Thessalonians, Paul remained in Athens. When he "could stand it no longer," he succeeded in sending Timothy to strengthen and encourage them in the faith (verses 1-2). Paul's primary concern (verse 3) was that their faith not be shaken by their afflictions (1Thessalonians 1.6, 3.7; 2 Thessalonians 1.4, 6; cf. 2.2). The articular noun, τῆς πίστεως ὑμῶν, "your faith," (verse 2) denoted what they had believed, Paul's instruction.

No one was more intimately aware than Paul of the ongoing cosmic battle of good against evil, some seen and some hidden. Satan's master plan against humanity is deception, a magic show. Satan presents a counterfeit, false reality to humanity. Angelic beings who followed him in his rebellion against God are his allies along with humans. Most humans are Satan's unwitting allies but some consciously follow and acknowledge him as master.

Paul wrote the Corinthians,

> [3] But if our gospel has been hidden, it has been hidden to those who perish, [4] in whom the god of this age blinded the minds of those who do not believe, so the light of the glorious gospel of the Christ, who is *the* image of the God, might not shine forth (2 Corinthians 4.3-4).

Satan, "the god of this age," ὁ θεὸς τοῦ αἰῶνος τούτου, blinds mankind to truth through a theater of deceit Paul called "the ruling forces of the world," τὰ στοιχεῖα τοῦ κόσμου (Galatians 4.3, 9; Colossians 2.8, 20). The noun στοιχεῖον refers to elements or basic principles such as the alphabet, elements, heavenly bodies, fundamental tenets of mathematics and science. Paul used the phrase, τὰ στοιχεῖα τοῦ κόσμου, to denote the world system Satan controls. He declared believers were once enslaved and in bondage to this system or "forces," but Christ had freed us from them. He warned his readers not to be captured again by them and described them as weak and destitute.

Everyone is aware of good and evil but most do not understand the source and main causality of evil is largely invisible—from Satan and those loyal to him. Satan wages a multi-layered, massive psychological operation against humanity to disguise truth and reality. Its genius is that most do not know exists.

When a person comes to know Christ, Satan directs his attack to draw one away from obeying and following Christ. Satan is a determined, powerful enemy who thinks he can defeat God. He will never repent or surrender. The Lord won the strategic victory over Satan by His death and resurrection. His tactical victory will occur in two phases. The first is at the end of the Tribulation (Revelation 19.11-20.3) and the final victory will be at the end of the Millennial kingdom (Revelation 20.7-10). Paul's most well-known instructions to us regarding our combat were written to the Ephesians:

> [10] As to the rest my brethren, be empowered in *the* Lord and in the strength of His might.
> [11] Put on the full armor of the God, so you

> can stand against the schemes of the Devil. [12] For our struggle is not against blood and flesh but against the rulers, against the authorities, against the cosmic lords of the darkness of this age, against the spiritual forces of the evil in the heavenlies. [13] Because of this, take up the full armor of the God, so you can withstand in this evil day, and when you have done everything, to stand. [14] Therefore, stand, by fastening your waist with truth and by putting on the breastplate of the righteousness, [15] and by having the feet shod in preparation of the gospel of the peace. [16] In everything, take up the shield of the faith, by which you can extinguish all the flaming arrows of the evil one. [17] And take the helmet of the salvation, and the sword of the Spirit, which is *the* word of God (Ephesians 6.10-17).

Paul taught the Thessalonians they would suffer for the Lord and this had occurred (verse 4). Despite these afflictions, he instructed them the Lord would rescue them from the Tribulation (1 Thessalonians 1.10).

Shrewd and subtle, Satan uses false teachers and false teachings to confuse and subvert God's message of love and grace. We must be constantly reminded and strengthened by the Scriptures lest we be deceived, entrapped, and stumble. Paul knew this from his own experience (cf. Romans 7) and from ministering to others. Paul would write in his last letter that everyone in Asia deserted him (2 Timothy 1.15). This is an astonishing statement given the time and effort he had spent ministering in Ephesus, Colossae, Iconium, Derbe, Lystra, Galatia, Antioch Pisidia, etc. It shows the formidable nature of Satan's false narrative and the dedication of his agents.

Knowing these things, and deeply concerned about the Thessalonians, Paul wrote, "Because of this, when I could stand it no longer, I sent so I might know about your faith, lest somehow the one who is tempting you somehow tempted you and our labor would be for nothing" (verse 5).

In verse 5, Paul repeated his statement in verse 1 that he could "stand it no longer," showing how concerned about them. This verse reveals that Paul learned that someone was attempting to lead the Thessalonians astray and that all his instruction would be in vain. Such concerns are just as real today as in Paul's time.

Tragically, the vast majority in Christendom, in seminaries, pulpits, and congregations are largely ignorant of the Bible as a whole and have little understanding of Church doctrine. Indeed, many churches wholly avoid Paul's letters. How can one understand Church theology if one avoids Paul's letters which contain *all* Church doctrine? The truth of this disunity and confusion is the existence of thousands of denominations.

Timothy's Encouraging Report

6 But now, Timothy came to us from you and brought good news to us of your faith and love and that you always have *a* good memory of us, constantly longing to see us, even as we also you.
7 Because of this, brethren, we were encouraged about you, in all our affliction and distress,[1] through your faith.
8 For now we live—if you stand fast in *the* Lord.
9 For what thanks can we give to the God about you for all the joy with which we rejoice because of you before our God?
10 We pray earnestly, night and day, that we might see your face and complete the things lacking in your faith.

Comment:

Verses 6-10: Happily, thankfully, Timothy returned to give Paul an encouraging report—the Thessalonians were holding to the faith, their love was strong, they had a good memory of Paul, and wished to see him

---

[1] Some manuscripts reverse the nouns, "in our distress and affliction," τῇ ἀνάγκῃ καὶθλίψει ἡμῶν.

(verse 6). This news cheered Paul in his own distress and affliction (verse 7). Paul was buoyed through their faith (διὰ τῆς ὑμῶν πίστεως). Nothing cheers a godly minister more than learning that believers to whom he has ministered are holding to the faith and growing in truth and love. Paul expressed this cheer as "living"—"for now we live—if you stand fast in *the* Lord," ὅτι νῦν ζῶμεν ἐὰν ὑμεῖς στήκητε ἐν κυρίῳ (verse 8).

Members of the Church compose the body of Christ as individuals, united. All parts are needed. Paul described this great truth to the Corinthians:

> 12 For as the body is one and has many members, and all the members of the one body, being many, are one body, so too *is* the Christ. 13 For by one Spirit we were all baptized into one body, whether Jews or Greeks, whether servants or freemen, and all were made to drink one Spirit. 14 For the body is not one member, but many (1 Corinthians 12.12-14).

> 24 Now our praiseworthy parts do not have *this* need. But the God composed the body by giving greater honor to the *parts* which are inferior, 25 so that there may be no division in the body, but that the members may have the same concern for one another. 26 So if one member suffers, all the members suffer with *it*. If *one* member is honored, all the members celebrate with *it*. 27 Now you are *the* body of Christ and members in particular (1 Corinthians 12.24-27).

Since we are a united organism, we should encourage believers who are troubled and suffer and celebrate with those who rejoice.

How much Paul was encouraged by the Thessalonians faith is further seen by his words in verse 9, where he rhetorically asked, "what thanks can we give to the God about you for all the joy with which we rejoice because of you before our God?" Like Paul, we should give thanks and rejoice when we see fellow believers growing in God's grace.

As a result of Timothy's good news, Paul wrote he prayed "earnestly, night and day" to see them and wished to "complete the things lacking in your faith," καταρτίσαι τὰ ὑστερήματα τῆς πίστεως ὑμῶν (verse 10). The verb καταρτίζω, translated "complete," means to bring something to its proper conclusion or condition. Paul used this verb seven other times (Romans 9.22; 1 Corinthians 1.10; 2 Corinthians 13.11; Galatians 6.1; Hebrews 10.5, 11.3, 13.21).

What did he mean by "complete the things lacking" in their faith? The main content of 1 Thessalonians is the Pre-Tribulational Rapture, Paul's focus when he was with them. Other things Paul wished to teach were the secrets the Lord revealed—the Church as the body of Christ, identification with Christ in His death and resurrection, living under grace rather than Law, the blinding of Israel, etc. As the Pre-Tribulation Rapture was a secret (1 Corinthians 15.51), Paul explained other secrets throughout his letters. They provide a full understanding of our position in Christ as members of the Church and God's plan and purposes.

Such words should motivate all who minister. The more one understands God's word, the greater one can appreciate who God is and praise Him for what He has done and what He will do. Such knowledge should strengthen believers to live godly lives.

As will be seen in 2 Thessalonians, Paul repeated what he had taught and written the Thessalonians about the Pre-Tribulation Rapture and enlarged on the advent of the Beast. His reply was required due to a false report they had received that their afflictions meant they were in the Tribulation.

---

[11] Now how we wish that our God and Father Himself and our Lord Jesus Christ, to direct our way to you.

12 And how we wish the Lord to increase and abound
you in the love for one another and for everyone, even
as we also for you,
13 so your hearts might be strengthened, blameless in
holiness before our God and Father at the coming of
our Lord Jesus Christ with all His saints.

Comment:

Verses 11-13: In verse 11, Paul expressed his wish "that our God and Father Himself and our Lord Jesus Christ, to direct our way to you," that the Lord would give him wisdom to understand their needs and guide him in ministering.

Having expressed continually prayer for the Thessalonians (verse 10), Paul continued in verses 11-13 to relay his wishes for them. These verses are an excellent guide for all believers, especially those who minister God's word. They reveal the following:

1. Asking God for guidance and direction in how to minister (verse 11).
2. Asking the Lord to increase and abound believers in Christian love for one another and for everyone, even as the one who ministers loves believers (verse 12).
3. Having the goal for hearts to be strengthened, to be blameless in holiness before God when the Lord returns with all His saints (verse 13).

These are part of sanctification. Most of the time Paul used the noun ἁγιασμός for the process of sanctification (cf. Romans 6.19, 22; 1 Corinthians 1.30; 1 Thessalonians 4.3-4, 7; 2 Thessalonians 2.13; 1 Timothy 2.15; Hebrews 12.14) or the verb ἁγιάζω (cf. Romans 15.16; 1 Corinthians 1.2, 6.11, 7.14; Ephesians 5.26; 1 Thessalonians 5.23; 1 Timothy 4.5; 2 Timothy 2.21; Hebrews 2.11, 9.13, 10.10, 14, 29, 13.12. In verse 13, however, he chose the noun ἁγιωσύνη, "holiness" or "sanctification." This noun is used only by Paul (cf. Romans 1.4; 2 Corinthians 7.1; 1 Thessalonians 3.13) and denotes holiness as condition and quality, our status in being set apart to

God. Adding σύνη to adjectives (here, ἅγιος, "holy," "set apart") is the means of forming abstract feminine nouns (e.g., αγράμματος, "illiterate" + σύνη for αγραμματοσύνη, "illiteracy"; δίκαιος, "righteous" + σύνη for δικαιοσύνη, "righteousness").

1 Thessalonians 4

Live to Please God

1 Therefore, brethren, as to the rest, we ask and urge
you in *the* Lord Jesus that as you received from us how
you must walk and please God (as you are walking)[1]
that you should abound even more.
2 For you know what commands we gave you through
the Lord Jesus.
3 For this is *the* will of the God—your sanctification:
that you abstain from the sexual immorality,
4 that each of you know how to control his own vessel
in holiness and honor,
5 not in lustful passion as the Gentiles, who do not
know the God,
6 that no one might take advantage of and defraud his
brother in the matter, because *the* Lord is *an* avenger
about all these things, even as we previously told and
testified to you.
7 For the God did not call us for impurity but in
holiness.
8 Consequently, the one who rejects *this* does not reject
man, but the God, the One who also gives us[2] His Holy
Spirit.

Comment:

Verses 1-8: Paul's expression "as to the rest," τὸ λοιπὸν, mark a close of what he had written above, verses 1-12 conclude what he wrote in chapters 1-3. When Paul first visited the Thessalonians and they believed his gospel, he instructed them about how to live "in (or by) Christ." He reminded them of this and urged them to continue to please God, as they were doing, and to excel in this even more (verse 1).

Each day is a journey with God. George MacDonald wrote "God is easy to please, but hard to satisfy." We must continue to advance toward our destiny as God's heirs, trusting Him. William Tyndale wrote, "When

---

[1] Some manuscripts do not have καθὼς καὶ περιπατεῖτε, "as you are walking."
[2] Some manuscripts have "you," ὑμᾶς.

God buildeth, He casteth all downe first. He is no patcher." God does not repair our fallen nature but gives us a new one. Our destiny is to become new creatures, free from sin and death, "conformed to the image of His Son" (Romans 8.29). Paul wrote the Corinthians,

> And as we bore the image of the earthly, we will also bear the image of the heavenly (1 Corinthians 15.49).

> Now we all, with unveiled face, as we view the glory of the Lord as in *a* mirror, we are transformed to the same image, from glory to glory, even as from *the* Lord, *the* Spirit (2 Corinthians 3.18)

In verse 2, Paul reminded the Thessalonians that his commands were through the Lord Jesus, διὰ τοῦ κυρίου Ἰησοῦ. Sometimes people say, "I follow Jesus, not Paul." Almost always they mean they follow what Jesus said in His earthly ministry. Do they not realize Jesus ministered only to Jews (with a couple exceptions) and operated under the Mosaic Law? Do they think they are under the Mosaic Law with its 613 commands? Do they realize the Mosaic Law was bondage (Acts 15.10; Galatians 4.22-31). Do they not realize the source of all Scripture is the Lord Jesus Christ? He is the Word of God, the Communicator. Was what God gave the prophets less authoritative than Jesus' words on earth? Paul wrote, "all Scripture is God-breathed" (2 Timothy 3.16), not just what Jesus spoke in His earthly ministry. Jesus ministered to Jews under the Mosaic Law, not to the Church, the body of Christ. How could He speak to the Church when did not yet exist? As shown above, the Scriptures reveal God began the Church with Paul.

Thus, all Paul wrote came from the ascended Lord (verse 2). When he penned something that did not come directly from the Lord, he noted it. For example, he wrote the Corinthians:

> Now this I say by way of permission, not after *a* command (1 Corinthians 7.6)

> Now about the virgins, I do not have *a* command from *the* Lord. But I give counsel which is trustworthy as one who has received mercy from the Lord (1 Corinthians 7.25).

Paul did not receive direct instruction from the Lord about these marriage questions. Nevertheless, what he wrote is Scripture, God-breathed, written under the control of the Holy Spirit and carry Christ's authority. To the Corinthians, Paul wrote, "If anyone thinks he is *a* prophet, or spiritual, he must recognize the things that I write to you are the commands of the Lord (1 Corinthians 14.37). Therefore, for members of the Church, to follow Christ is to follow the words of Paul.

In verse 3, Paul declared God's will was for believers to be sanctified, "your sanctification," ὁ ἁγιασμὸς ὑμῶν. Paul addressed two areas in verses 3-6: sexual morality and personal integrity. Regarding the former, Paul urged the Thessalonians to exercise control and abstain from the sexual immorality practiced by Gentiles.

As a result of being "in Adam," we inherit a fallen nature inclined toward immorality. The ancient world's religious systems institutionalized sexual immorality in the worship of false gods and idolatry. Every culture and civilization had gods, which were essentially the same, but known by different names and stories. Female goddesses were called Asherah, Artemis, Diana, Aphrodite, etc. Male gods were known as Baal, Zeus, Pan, Dionysius. Pagan theology taught that cultic sexual relations influenced the gods to give the people children and good harvests. "Priestesses," essentially prostitutes, represented female goddesses in the temples. The Greek geographer Strabo wrote about 2 B.C. that Corinth's temple of Aphrodite was so wealthy that it owned more than a thousand prostitutes. Whether this was true in Paul's day is unclear but "sacred" prostitution and sexual immorality still pervaded society.

That most of the believing Thessalonians were Gentiles is clear from Paul's statement in 1 Thessalonians 1.9—they "turned to the God from the idols to serve *the* living and true God." They had been Gentiles—but were no longer. Now they had a new identity: Church, members of the body of Christ.

After God called Abraham and established the Abrahamic Covenant, He divided humanity into two theological groups: Jews and Gentiles. When God saved and commissioned Paul, He created a third theological group: the Church, the body of Christ. Three theological groups presently exist: Jew, Gentile, and Church (1 Corinthians 10.32).

One who believes Paul's gospel (1 Corinthians 15.1-4) whether Jew or Gentile, becomes a new creation: Church—a member of Christ's body with a new identity, no longer Jew or Gentile. Thus, Paul wrote:

> Therefore, if anyone *is* in Christ: *a* new creation. The old things passed away. Behold, new things have come into being (2 Corinthians 5.17.

The Church is this "new creation" and one acquires a new identity as being a member of it. The "old things," one's former nature "in Adam," one's former identity as "Jew" or "Gentile," have passed away "in Christ." Thus, Paul wrote the Corinthians and Galatians:

> For as all in the Adam die, so too all in the Christ will be made alive (1 Corinthians 15.22).

> There is no Jew or Greek, there is no servant or freeman, there is no male and female. For you are all one in Christ Jesus (Galatians 3.28).

> For in Christ Jesus neither circumcision nor uncircumcision avails anything: Instead, a new creation (Galatians 6.15).

Similarly, Paul wrote the Colossians:

> [9] Do not lie to one another, since you put off the old man with his practices, [10] and since you put on the new, the one who is being renewed in full knowledge, after *the* image of the One who created him, [11] where there is no Greek and Jew, circumcision and uncircumcision, foreigner, Scythian, servant, freeman. Rather, Christ is everything, and in everything (Colossians 3.9-11).

On the day God completes the Church, He will remove it from earth. Two theological groups will remain on earth, Jew and Gentile. They will undergo the Tribulation, part of God's prophetic plan that concerns Israel and the nations (Gentiles). Since the Church is outside prophecy, God must remove it to restart His prophetic plan.

Paul continued his exhortation in verses 4 and 5, writing, "that each of you know how to control his own vessel in holiness and honor, not in lustful passion as the Gentiles, who do not know the God." Gentiles did not know the true God because they accepted and worshipped false gods. With few exceptions, Gentiles lived according to "the ruling forces of the world," τὰ στοιχεῖα τοῦ κόσμου (Galatians 4.3, 9; Colossians 2.8, 20), Satan's religious theater of deceit.

Paul urged them not to live after their old identities as Gentiles who did not know God, (verse 5) but to live as God's new creation as Church, members of Christ's body, "in holiness and honor" (verse 4). Paul used the imagery of one's body being a "vessel," σκεῦος, (verse 4) in several passages (Romans 9.22-23; 2 Corinthians 4.7; 2 Timothy 2.21) and the Lord told Ananias, "Go. For this man is *a* chosen vessel (σκεῦος) to Me, to carry My name before the Gentiles, and kings, and the sons of Israel" (Acts 9.15).

Paul continued his exhortation regarding sexual immorality in verse 6, telling the Thessalonians not to take advantage of and defraud one's brother "in the matter," ἐν τῷ πράγματι, that is, in sexual immorality.

An adulterer defrauds spouse and children. One who commits fornication defrauds one's future spouse and children. Both defraud their illicit partner. Paul reminded them he had "told and testified" to them that the Lord is an avenger of these things. The adjective translated "avenger," ἔκδικος, is used twice in the New Testament, both by Paul. In Romans 13.4, he used it for rulers who punish lawbreakers.

Writing the Corinthians, Paul warned about judgment of a believer for sexual immorality (1 Corinthians 5.1-8) and counseled them, "Clean out the old yeast so you may be *a* new lump, since you are unleavened" (1 Corinthians 5.7).

God has called members of His Church to holiness, not impurity (verse 7; cf. 1 Corinthians 6.9-11). Those who rejected Paul's warnings did not reject him but God (verse 8), who has given us the Holy Spirit, God's down payment that we are His heirs (1 Corinthians 1.22; 2 Corinthians 5.5; Ephesians 1.14).

---

[9] Now about the brotherly love, you have no need *for me* to write to you, for you yourselves are divinely instructed to love one another.
[10] And you are doing this to all the brethren, the ones in all Macedonia. But we urge you brethren to abound even more,
[11] and to strive to live quietly, and to attend to your own *business,* and to work with your own hands, as we commanded you
[12] so you may walk properly towards outsiders and so no one may have need.

Comment:

Verses 9-12: Finishing his exhortation for believers not to engage in sexual immorality, Paul turned to the subject of brotherly love. He declared they did not need him to write them about this for they were taught by God to love one another (verse 9) and that they were practicing love to all the brethren in Macedonia (verse 10). As usual, Paul urged them to abound in love even more. Room for improvement always exists.

Paul also encouraged them to live quietly, attend to their own business, and work with their own hands (verse 11). Paul did this himself, working to provide for his own needs while he was with them. Godly living includes managing one's own life rather than interfering and trying to control the lives of others.

Believers fail in the faith by being busybodies. Jesus instructed believers to remove the beam from their eye before addressing the splinter in another's (Matthew 7.1-5). Paul also wished that they "walk properly towards outsiders," unbelievers, and not be dependent on them. God has set the Church apart for Himself and members of His body should take care of one another as much as possible rather than relying on those outside the faith.

Christ's Return for His Church: the Rapture

13 Now I do not want you to be ignorant, brethren,
about those who have fallen asleep, so that you may
not grieve as the rest, those who have no hope.
14 For if we believe that Jesus died and rose, so also,
the God will bring with Him those who fell asleep
through Jesus.
15 For we say this to you by *the* word of *the* Lord, that
we who remain alive until the Lord comes, should not
precede those who fell asleep.
16 For the Lord Himself, with *a* commanding shout,
with *the* voice of *an* archangel and with *the* trumpet of
God, will descend from heaven. And the dead in Christ
will rise first.
17 Then, we who remain alive, will be caught up with
them in *the* clouds to meet the Lord in *the* air. And so,
we will always be with *the* Lord.
18 Therefore, encourage one another with these words.

Comment:

Verses 13-18: These verses through Chapter 5.1-11 contain the main doctrinal content of the letter. Paul began, declaring he did not want the Thessalonians to be ignorant (ἀγνοεῖν) about those who had fallen asleep. God does not want His children to be ignorant and has provided His word so that we may know His plan and will. Paul used the verb "sleep," κοιμάομαι, as a euphemism for physical death of believers (1 Corinthians 11.30, 15.6, 18, 20, 51; 1 Thessalonians 4.13, 14,15). At death, the physical body is "asleep," awaiting resurrection. Jesus taught there are two general resurrections, one to life and one to condemnation (John 5.28-29). Paul detailed the order of the Church's resurrection here and in 1 Corinthians 15. Old Testament believers and those killed in the Tribulation have a separate resurrection from the Church and are resurrected after the Tribulation to inhabit the kingdom (Daniel 12.11-13).

The body is resurrected from "sleep." Immaterial soul and spirit never sleep for they need no rest and cannot die. The Bible indicates no time of unconsciousness for soul or spirit. They are always awake and aware. When a believer dies, his soul and spirit go to be with the Lord (2 Corinthians 5.8, 12.2-4; Philippians 1.23-24), awaiting reunion with the body. In Jewish and Christian thought, we are incomplete without body, soul, and spirit. All three compose our being made in God's image (1 Thessalonians 5.23; Genesis 1.27).

Paul wanted the Thessalonian believers to understand the status of members the Church who had died so they might not grieve, "as the rest, the ones who have no hope," οἱ λοιποὶ οἱ μὴ ἔχοντες ἐλπίδα. "The rest," those with "no hope," are unbelievers. God gives every person a lifetime of opportunities to choose for or against Him. Every second of one's life is an opportunity for it only takes a second to believe the gospel. Physical death ends those opportunities. Tragically, few choose to respond to God. Jesus spoke solemnly about this subject:

> 13 Enter through the narrow gate. For wide *is* the gate and broad the way leading to the destruction. And many are the ones who enter through it. 14 For the gate *is* narrow and the way is difficult that leads to the life.

> And few are the ones who find it (Matthew 7.13-14).

Most of humanity spurn Christ's love and salvation. Many believe God will accept them on their own terms. The first example of this attitude was Cain, who approached God with a sacrifice of his harvest from the ground, rather than an animal sacrifice which God specified (Genesis 4.2-7). God tells us how we must come to Him. To reject His way rejects Him. Those who reject Christ will stand before Him with only their own righteousness rather than His all-sufficient righteousness (John 5.22, 27; Revelation 20.11-15). Like Cain, it is insufficient.

Paul declared God's way of salvation—"if we believe that Jesus died and rose"—his gospel (verse 14)—how one is saved today, how one becomes a Christian, how one becomes a member of the Church, the body of Christ. More fully, he wrote the Corinthians:

> [1] Now I declare to you, brethren, the gospel that I proclaimed to you, which you also received, by which also you stand, [2] through which also you are saved, if you possess that message I proclaimed to you, unless you believed in vain. [3] For I delivered to you first what I also received: Christ died for our sins, according to the Scriptures, [4] and that He was buried, and that He has been raised on the third day, according to the Scriptures (1 Corinthians 15.1-4).

Could salvation be simpler? How is one saved from sin and death? One must believe Christ died for one's sins and rose from the dead. Period. Most of humanity rejects this simple message. Most think they can approach God on their own terms and He will accept them. Solomon wrote:

> There is a way that seems right to a man, but the end thereof are the ways of death (Proverbs 16.25).

Jesus declared,

> I am the way, and the truth, and the life. No one comes to the Father except through Me (John 14.6).

Paul comforted the Thessalonians by writing that God would bring believers who had died, "those who fell asleep through Jesus," τοὺς κοιμηθέντας διὰ τοῦ Ἰησοῦ. God knows each of us as His children. Such phrasing softened the pain of death. Those who had died were with Christ (their souls and spirits) while their bodies "slept" awaiting resurrection.

In verse 15, Paul continued to explain how this resurrection will work. He declared, "we say this to you by *the* word of *the* Lord." What did this mean? Like his gospel, this information came directly from the ascended Christ. Paul wrote regarding the gospel,

> [11] Now I declare to you brethren, the gospel I proclaimed is not after man. [12] For I neither received nor was taught from man but through revelation of Jesus Christ (Galatians 1.11-12).

What Paul wrote the Thessalonians about the Pre-Tribulation Rapture was part of the revelation package he called secrets—truths the ascended Lord revealed to him alone, truths God had kept hidden.

In verse 15, Paul declared that believers who are alive when the Lord comes will not precede those who have died. His "not" statement is the double negative οὐ μὴ with the subjunctive, the strongest negation.

Verse 16 describes how this great event will occur. The Lord of Hosts, the Lord Jesus Christ, will initiate it with a commanding shout. An archangel will echo His command and the trumpet of God will sound. This is. This sequence, how military commands have been given for millennia, signals the Lord's descent from heaven.

Before proceeding, a comment must be made about "*the* trumpet of God," σάλπιγγι θεοῦ, i.e., "God's trumpet." The first thing to note is that it is a singular trumpet, not one in a series. As such, it is distinct from "the seven trumpets," τὰς ἑπτὰ σάλπιγγας, described in Revelation 8.6. Those trumpets belong to angels, not described as God's trumpet. They are blown sequentially, not singularly, as is God's.

The trumpets sounded in Revelation signal God's judgments on the earth. They echo the seven trumpets blown by the priests in Israel's attack of Jericho under Joshua (Joshua 6.4, 6, 8, 13) that signaled war. God's trumpet that Paul describes does not signal war but blessing—the resurrection of members of the Church, the body of Christ. No judgment is associated with this trumpet.

God's trumpet is outside the events of Revelation. Revelation contains no mention and no hint of the Church, the body of Christ. It reveals God's prophetic plan for Israel and the nations (Gentiles).

The parallel passage to 1 Thessalonians 4.13-18 is 1 Corinthians 15, which reads:

> 51 Behold! I tell you *a* secret: we will not all sleep but we will all be changed— 52 in *an* instant, in *the* blink of *an* eye, at the last trumpet. For *the* trumpet will sound and the dead will be raised incorruptible. Then, we will be changed. 53 For this corruptible *body* must put on incorruption and this mortal must put on immortality. 54 Now when this corruptible should put on incorruption, and this mortal puts on immortality, then will come to pass the word which has been written: The death was swallowed up in victory.

Paul described the event as a secret, μυστήριον, "Behold, I tell you a secret," ἰδού, μυστήριον ὑμῖν λέγω. The noun μυστήριον begins the text to emphasize it being a secret. This truth is never mentioned in the Old Testament, in the Gospels, or in the writings of Peter, James, John, and Jude. It was a secret the ascended Lord gave Paul alone. As a secret, it belongs to a new set of revelations, which apply to the Church, which was also a secret. It is therefore, outside God's prophetic plan of the Tribulation and Christ's Second Advent, which were known.

What was the secret Paul revealed? He declared not all members of the Church will sleep, that is, die. All, however, will be changed—whether alive or dead. Jesus spoke of the resurrection of life (John 5.24-29) and members of the Church are part of this resurrection. What Paul revealed was new—the Church's resurrection is separate from the resurrection of Old Testament believers and some will escape physical death. They will be instantly transformed, exchanging mortal bodies for immortal ones.

Paul wrote this will occur "at the last trumpet," ἐν τῇ ἐσχάτῃ σάλπιγγι. Some argue the "last trumpet" is the seventh trumpet of Revelation 11.15-19. As explained above, this is theologically impossible. The Church is outside prophecy, for it is a new creation God kept hidden. Too many differences exist for the trumpet Paul described to be the seventh trumpet of Revelation. Indeed, *nothing* in Revelation fits Paul's description. The seventh trumpet of Revelation announces Christ's reign on earth and is associated with His Second Advent, which were known events, not what Paul revealed—a secret. What then did Paul mean by his phrase, "the last trumpet?"

Paul only mentioned *one* trumpet with reference to the Church, described as "the last trumpet," τῇ ἐσχάτῃ σάλπιγγι (1 Corinthians 15.52). As such, "last" cannot mean "last" in a series like the trumpets in Revelation 8.6-11.15. Rather, "last," ἔσχατος means last in the sense of signaling completion. The adjective, ἔσχατος, has two basic senses. One denotes a final event in a succession or a series. The other denotes last as an end or completion. Jesus declared He was the "Alpha and Omega, the First and the Last (Revelation 1.11, 17, 22.13). He did not mean He was "last" in a series, but "last" in that He was the Completer, the Finisher.

Paul used ἔσχατος in the latter sense. The "last trumpet" sounds to signal completion—completion of the Church. When the last person believes Paul's gospel, which completes the Church, the body of Christ, the Lord sounds the trumpet of God, announcing His Church has been completed.

Once complete, Christ gives all Church members resurrection bodies and removes those who are alive from earth. Since the Church, the body of Christ, is a united organism, we must receive resurrection bodies at the same time. Believers who are alive when this occurs will not experience physical death. It would make no sense for members of the Church who are alive to die and then be immediately resurrected. While the vast majority of humanity suffers physical death, the consequence of Adam's sin, one generation of believers does not.

Paul wrote, "it is appointed to mankind to die once" (Hebrews 9.27) but this does not mean everyone must die. That is our fate "in Adam" but all "in Christ" will be made alive (1 Corinthians 15.22). Jesus Christ can intervene and bypass the consequence of physical death for He is Lord of heaven and earth, the Firstborn from the dead. That is what occurs at the Rapture. God intervenes and those "in Christ" do not experience physical death.

The articular construction, "the dead in Christ," οἱ νεκροὶ ἐν Χριστῷ, in verse 16 identified members of the Church, the body of Christ, who had died. These are the same "the dead," οἱ νεκροὶ, Paul described in 1 Corinthians 15.52. Paul stated "they will rise first," ἀναστήσονται πρῶτον.[3]

Paul continued in verse 17, writing, "we who remain alive will be caught up with them in the clouds to meet the Lord in the air." Again, Paul's language, "we who remain alive" indicated he expected to experience the Rapture in his lifetime.

---

[3] This is an example of how Paul used the adjective πρῶτός, always "first." See discussion in 1 Thessalonians 1 about Paul being "first" not "worst."

Paul then stated that those who are alive "will be caught up." The verb translated "caught up" is ἁρπάζω. Paul used this verb in a technical sense: to be translated into the Lord's presence (cf. 2 Corinthians 12.2, 4). Literally, the verb ἁρπάζω means "snatched" or "caught away" (cf. Matthew 13.19; John 6.15, 10.12; Acts 8.39; 2 Corinthians 12.2, 4). This word has come to be known as "Rapture." Why is this? When St. Jerome (c. 347-420 A.D.) revised the Latin New Testament, he translated ἁρπάζω with the Latin "rapiemur." When this verb was transliterated into English, it became our word "rapture." While ἁρπάζω is used only here to describe the Pre-Tribulation Rapture, Paul taught the Pre-Tribulation Rapture in other passages with other vocabulary. This "snatching" by the Lord removes His Church from His wrath, the judgments of the Tribulation that will shortly commence (Romans 5.9; 1 Thessalonians 1.10, 5.9; Colossians 1.13).

What are the "clouds" of verse 17? Did Paul mean the clouds in the sky, rain clouds? In addition to the normal meaning of rain clouds, both Hebrew, עָב, and Greek, νεφέλη, nouns describe the heavenly host and God's glory. Consider the following passages:

> I will ascend above the heights of the clouds; I will be like the most High (Isaiah 14.14).
>
> I saw in the night visions, and, behold, one like the Son of man came with the clouds of heaven, and came to the Ancient of days, and they brought him near before him (Daniel 7.14).
>
> While he was still speaking, behold, *a* bright cloud overshadowed them. And behold, *a* voice spoke from the cloud, saying, This is My Beloved Son, in whom I delight. Listen to Him (Matthew 17.5).
>
> And then the sign of the Son of the Man will appear in the heaven. And then all the peoples of the earth will mourn. And they will see the Son of the Man coming on the

> clouds of the heaven with great power and glory (Matthew 24.30).
>
> Then Jesus said, I am. And you will see the Son of the Man sitting at the right hand of the Power and coming with the clouds of the heaven (Mark 14.62).
>
> And after He said these things, while they watched, He was taken up. And *a* cloud received Him from their eyes (Acts 1.9).
>
> Behold, He comes with the clouds. And every eye will see Him, even those who pierced Him. And all the peoples of the earth will wail because of Him. Yes! Amen (Revelation 1.7)!

Isaiah 14.13-14 records Satan's thoughts. He did not state he would ascend above rain clouds (verse 14) but planned to take God's place above the angelic host and be like God. The other passages declare the Lord's presence and coming with His heavenly host. So too the Rapture. When the Lord comes for His Church, He is surrounded by glory with His angelic host. Will this event be seen? No. It occurs in a split second, unlike when He comes at His Second Advent, when "every eye will see Him."

At this return of Christ, members of the Church who are alive are transformed, given resurrection bodies, to join resurrected believers who had died previously. Both meet the Lord in the air, εἰς ἀέρα, the sky. Thus, the Head of the body, Christ, is united with His completed body (Ephesians 5.23; Colossians 1.18, 2.19; cf. 1 Corinthians 12.12-27). The noun ἀήρ, denotes the lower atmosphere or sky as opposed to αἰθήρ, which denotes the upper atmosphere, space, or heaven. The result of this meeting is "we will always be with *the* Lord." Is any blessing greater than this? Nothing is greater than to be with the Lord, to be with the One who loves us, who gave Himself for us, who created us in His image. His presence is eternal joy.

Paul expected to experience the Rapture, which is why he wrote "we who remain alive." Unlike the Twelve, who expected to undergo the Tribulation and see Christ at His Second Advent, Paul expected to be rescued from that judgment with other members of the Church who are alive.

Many passages attest to the belief that the apostles thought the Lord would return in their lifetime (Matthew 3.1-2, 4.17, 10.5-7, 16.28, 24.32-35, 26.62-64; John 21.22-23; Acts 2.14-21, 3.19-21; Romans 3.11-12; 1 Corinthians 1.4-8, 10.11, 15.51-52; 1 Thessalonians 4.13-17; Hebrews 10.24-25, 36-37; James 5-7-8; 1 Peter 1.3-6, 4.7; 1 John 2.18; Jude 1.17-18; Revelation 1.1-3, 22.6-7, 22.10-12).

Paul's words in verses 16 and 17 parallel what he wrote the Corinthians in 1 Corinthians 15.51-52. Both declare:

1. Not all members of the Church will die.
2. The Church's resurrection is announced by a trumpet.
3. Members of the Church who have died are raised first.
4. Members of the Church who are alive are raised a split second later.
5. All members of the Church are united with Christ in the air.

Paul concluded the chapter (verse 18), "Therefore, encourage one another with these words." What does this mean? It means individual believers and churches are *commanded* to teach the Pre-Tribulational Rapture. The verb translated "encourage," παρακαλεῖτε, is a present active imperative. Paul's words were not a suggestion or wish but a command. Therefore, believers and churches who wish to obey Christ must teach the doctrine of the Pre-Tribulation Rapture and encourage fellow believers with it. If not, one fails to be faithful to Christ. Such a failure constitutes the "wood, hay, and stubble" at the Day of Christ when the Lord will examine or works and give rewards (1 Corinthians 3.12-15).

Excursus: Paul's Secrets

Many in Christendom have accepted the truth of the Pre-Tribulation Rapture but most do not recognize this truth was unrevealed and unknown before Paul. Because of this, some have seen a reference to the Rapture in passages like Matthew 24.40-41 and John 14.3. The Matthew passage reads,

> 40 Then two men will be in the field: one is taken and one is left. 41 Two women will be grinding in the mill: one is taken and one is left (Matthew 24.40-41).

Some think the one "taken" is the Rapture. But how could the Lord speak about the Rapture in His earthly ministry? It was a secret. The Rapture pertains to the Church, the body of Christ. Jesus could not speak about the Church for it did not yet exist. It too was a secret. Jesus, in His earthly ministry, addressed Jews about God's prophetic plan. Throughout Matthew 24 the Lord explained what will occur in the Tribulation and that He would return at its end. The Tribulation is Daniel's 70th week (Daniel 9.24), concerning Israel and the nations. The Lord's counsel to the disciples and to Israel was to endure to the end to be saved (Matthew 24.13). Some will endure and some will not. Thus, the one "taken" is one who does *not* endure but is taken to judgment. The one "left" is one who does endure and will enter the earthly kingdom and enjoy Christ's millennial reign.

The John passage reads:

> 2 In My Father's house are many dwellings. Now if not, I would have told you, for I go to prepare *a* place for you. 3 And if I should go on and prepare *a* place for you, I am coming again and will receive you to Myself—so where I am you may be also (John 14.2-3).

Many think this passage means the Lord is preparing "mansions" for His people and when ready, He will return and bring them to heaven to live. Such a view leads them to think this is a Rapture passage.

Again, how could the Lord speak of the Rapture when Paul wrote it was a secret? Something cannot be known and unknown. God has many "dwellings" and these include accommodations for His angelic host as well as humanity. As much as we try to protect homes and possessions, nothing is safe and secure in our present world. Because of this, the Lord counseled His followers not to accumulate treasures on earth but in heaven (Matthew 6.19-20).

When the Lord returns, those who believed the gospel of the kingdom during the Lord's earthly ministry and in the Tribulation and the Old Testament saints who believed in the God of the Bible as He revealed Himself will enjoy the treasures the Lord has kept safe in heaven and inhabit the dwellings He has prepared there to be enjoyed on earth. When the Lord reigns as King, earth becomes safe and secure.

Throughout the Gospels, the Lord instructed His disciples to prepare for the Tribulation and to enter the kingdom. The Lord's coming in John's passage is His Second Advent when He returns to earth as the two angels told His disciples in Acts 1.9-11 (cf. Zechariah 14.1-4). He will receive His saints to Himself on earth, not in the air (as the Rapture) or in heaven. Nothing in Jewish theology indicated Jews (or Gentiles) would go to heaven or live in heaven. Everything the prophets wrote, everything Jesus taught, indicated Jews and Gentiles who trusted in the God of the Bible would live on earth. Paul wrote, "Jesus Christ became *a* servant of *the* circumcision for *the* truth of God to confirm the promises of the fathers (Romans 15.8). Only in Paul's letters do we learn of people going to heaven and having heavenly citizenship (Philippians 3.20). This status is exclusive to members of the Church, the body of Christ, to those who believe Paul's gospel.

Thus, while many believe in the Pre-Tribulation Rapture, most do not understand it was a secret. The vast majority of seminary professors, theologians, pastors, and churchgoers have almost no knowledge or understanding of Paul's secrets. The Rapture was but one of several secrets Paul received from the ascended Lord. Thus, Paul wrote the Corinthians:

> So, let *a* man reckon us as officers of Christ and stewards of the secrets of God (1 Corinthians 4.1).

Paul and those who joined him in his ministry and apostleship were "stewards of the secrets of God." God revealed *several* secrets to Paul, things God had kept hidden, unrevealed in His prophetic plan.

When one reads Paul's letters and compares what he wrote with the Old Testament, Gospels, and letters of James, Peter, John, and Jude, one will realize almost *everything* Paul wrote was a secret—new revelation. The exception is when Paul wrote about prophecy, which he did rarely. When Paul did mention prophecy, it concerned God's wrath, the Tribulation, and the man of the lawlessness in 2 Thessalonians 2. He did this to reassure his readers that members of the Church would not experience the Tribulation for the Lord would remove them from earth before it began.

Before proceeding, the noun "secret," μυστήριον, should be examined. Translators have done shoddy work in rendering it "mystery." This mistranslation has sown great confusion for readers of the Bible. Our word "mystery" connotes what is strange or weird, something that baffles or eludes understanding. But a "secret" is something hidden or concealed. Once a secret is revealed, it is known and understood. This is the meaning of μυστήριον. The Rapture and Paul's other secrets were not things strange or weird, things that eluded understanding, but truths God kept hidden until He was ready to reveal them.

The proper time for God's disclosure of the Rapture was Paul's commission and apostleship for it concerned the Church, the body of Christ. This is why it cannot be found in the Old Testament, Gospels, or in the writings of James, Peter, John, or Jude.

As noted above, Paul mentioned more than one μυστήριον. What were they? Paul wrote the Romans the following:

> For I do not wish you to be ignorant brethren of this secret [μυστήριον]—so you may not be wise in yourselves—partial hardening has happened to Israel, until the completion of the Gentiles might enter in (Romans 11.25).

Israel's partial hardening was a secret. Such hardening was national, not a personal or individual. The Old Testament revealed no such hardening related to the Jews acceptance of their Messiah. The prophets wrote that the Messiah would be opposed but nothing indicated it would continue. Peter and the other apostles expected Israel to repent after Christ rose from the dead.

When one reads the prophets, it appears that once the Messiah came and the prophecies about Him began to be fulfilled, they would all be completed in short order. Paul thought the Church would be completed in his lifetime and he would experience the Rapture. Peter and the other apostles thought that while the Jews had rejected and crucified their Messiah the nation would repent and accept Him as Messiah and King. They thought the Tribulation would occur and He would return at its end and establish His kingdom. This is why they wrote again and again that Christ's return was near. They thought God would fulfill His covenant promises and Jews would fulfill their destiny as priests (Exodus 19.6; 1 Peter 2.9; Zechariah 8.20-23) and be the light of the Gentiles (Isaiah 42.6, 49.6) to bring Gentiles to Christ. The conversion of Gentiles would fulfill Jesus' evangelistic command in Acts 1.8, "and to the ends of the earth."

In Romans 11, Paul wrote Israel's national hardening would continue until "the completion of the Gentiles." With his illustration of the olive tree, he explained how God had put Gentiles into the place of divine blessing. Paul's expression, "the completion of the Gentiles" was the completion of the Church, the body of Christ.

Once complete, God would finish His prophetic program. Israel's national "hardening" was a secret.

Paul wrote the Ephesians:

> 1 For this reason, I Paul, the prisoner of Christ Jesus for you Gentiles, 2 seeing that you heard of the dispensation of the grace of the God, which was given to me for you, 3 that by revelation [ἀποκάλυψις] He made known to me the secret [μυστήριον], as I briefly wrote before, 4 by which, you can by reading understand my insight in the secret [μυστήριον] of the Christ, 5 which, in other generations, was not made known to the sons of men, as now was revealed to His holy apostles and prophets by *the* Spirit: 6 that the Gentiles should be joint heirs, and of the same body, and joint partakers of the promise in the Christ, through the gospel, 7 of which I became servant, according to the gift of the grace of God, which was given to me, according to the working of His power. 8 To me, to the least of all saints, was this grace given: to preach to the Gentiles the incomprehensible riches of the Christ, 9 and to enlighten everyone about the dispensation of the secret [μυστήριον], which has been hidden from the ages in the God, the One who created all things through Jesus Christ (Ephesians 3.8-9).

The Old Testament prophets revealed Gentiles would be blessed by and through Israel. God initiated this program when He made His covenant with Abraham (Genesis 12.1-3). Nothing in the prophets hinted that God would bless Gentiles apart from national Israel. Nothing in the Old Testament indicated God would create an organism in which Jew and Gentile were equal in Christ, indwelt by the Holy Spirit, saved by faith alone. When God saved and commissioned Paul everything changed. God created something entirely new, the Church, the body of Christ, a secret (verses 3, 4, 9) the Lord revealed to Paul alone (verses 2, 3, 6, 8).

What did Paul mean by "as now was revealed to His holy apostles and prophets by *the* Spirit." Did this include the Twelve? Paul likely meant the apostles and prophets who ministered with him. But if he also included the Twelve and those who ministered to Israel, they learned about the Church from Paul. The record of Acts makes it clear that the Twelve had no idea about the Church, the body of Christ, before the Lord revealed it to Paul. See the excursus, Did the Church Began at Pentecost? The Church, the body of Christ, was another secret the risen Lord revealed to Paul.

Paul wrote the Romans and Ephesians:

> Now to Him who can establish you according to my gospel, even the preaching of Jesus Christ according to secret [μυστήριον] revelation, which has been kept silent in *the* times in the ages (Romans 16.25).
>
> [18] Through every prayer and request, pray at all times in *the* Spirit, even for this very thing, watching with all perseverance and request for all the saints, and for me, so I might be given *a* message with boldness in opening my mouth, to make known the secret [μυστήριον] of the gospel (Ephesians 6.18-19).

Paul called the gospel he proclaimed "my gospel," so designated because it was new (cf. Romans 2.16; Galatians 2.2; 2 Timothy 2.8). The "gospel," God's good news of salvation, has changed over time. After Adam and Eve fell, God showed an animal sacrifice, shedding animal's blood, was required for salvation. Animal sacrifices became formalized under the Mosaic Law and until Paul, both faith and works were intertwined in salvation. Offering an animal sacrifice was a "work," but a work resulting from faith. Faith is obeying God. One exercises faith by doing what God said. This is what Paul meant by his expression "obedience of faith," ὑπακοὴν πίστεως, (Romans 1.5, 16.26).

During the Lord's earthly ministry and the ministry of the gospel of the kingdom, salvation required keeping the Law (Matthew 19.16-22), water baptism (Mark 1.4, 16.16; Acts 2.38, 22.16), forgiving sins (Matthew 6.12-15), and faith. The faith of the gospel of the kingdom was believing Jesus was the Christ, the Son of God (Matthew 16.16; John 1.49, 11.26-27; Acts 9.20).

What Paul proclaimed for salvation was entirely different from anything known before. This is why he wrote "the secret of the gospel," τὸ μυστήριον τοῦ εὐαγγελίου (Ephesians 6.19). The gospel of the kingdom that began with John the Baptist focused on Christ's *identity*, who He was, the Messiah, the Son of God. It was not a secret. Paul's gospel focused on Christ's *work*, He died for our sins and rose from the dead. Peter and the Twelve knew nothing about this gospel. Had Peter known it, he would have proclaimed it at Pentecost. Peter addressed only Jews at Pentecost. He did not tell them Christ died for their sins and rose from the dead and that by believing this one was saved. He told them that Jesus had risen from the dead but not as a message of salvation. Rather, he told them to repent from the sin of murdering Him, and be baptized (Acts 2.36-38).

As late as the Council of Jerusalem (51 A.D.), Acts reveals the Jewish leaders in Jerusalem did not understand Paul's gospel. They were telling Paul's converts they had to keep the Law and be circumcised to be saved. Paul wrote the Galatians that he had to explain his gospel to them. Had they understood Paul's gospel, had they been proclaiming it, this would have been unnecessary. Indeed, a council would not have been necessary.

Paul's gospel declared salvation by faith alone, which was previously unknown. Before Paul, faith and works were enmeshed, a warp and woof fabric. Abraham was an exception (Romans 4.1-5; cf. Genesis 15.1-6). Apart from this example, salvation required both faith and works.

Thus, Paul's gospel was a secret he received from the ascended Lord. He wrote the Galatians:

> [11] Now I declare to you brethren, the gospel I proclaimed is not after man. [12] For I neither received nor was taught from man but through revelation of Jesus Christ (Galatians 1.11-12).

These secrets were part of the revelatory package Paul received from the risen Lord. Unless one understands that Paul wrote about secrets he alone received from the risen Lord and that they constitute all Church theology, one cannot understand Church theology.

1 Thessalonians 5

The Day of the Lord

1 Now about the times and the seasons, brethren, you
have no need for me to write you.
2 For yourselves fully know that *the* day of *the* Lord
comes as *a* thief in *the* night.
3 For when they should say, Peace and security, then,
sudden destruction comes on them, as she who has the
labor pain in her womb. And they will not escape.
4 But you, brethren, are not in darkness, so the day
should overtake you as *a* thief.
5 For you all are sons of light and sons of day. We are
not of night or of darkness.
6 So then, we should not sleep as the others, but should
stay alert and be sober.
7 For the sleepers sleep at night. And the drunkards get
drunk at night.
8 But since we are of *the* day, we should be sober, by
putting on *the* breastplate of faith and love, and *the*
helmet—*the* hope of salvation.

Comment:

Verses 1-8: As he wrote in 1 Thessalonians 4.9, Paul declared they had no need for him to write to them "about the times and seasons," περὶ δὲ τῶν χρόνων καὶ τῶν καιρῶν (verse 1). The phrase, "times and seasons," occurs twice in the New Testament (cf. Acts 1.7). The nouns, "times," χρόνος and "seasons," καιρός, have distinct meanings: χρόνος is broader and embraces "seasons," καιροί, while the latter term refers to a specific period within the larger seriality of "time," χρόνος. Paul wrote he did not need to write them about this because he had taught this subject when he was with them. But having said this, he reminded them about it anyway. Thus, his statement was an idiom, "I know you know this, but am going to tell you anyway."

In verse 2, Paul reminded them of what they "fully knew," κριβῶς οἴδατε, "that the day of the Lord comes as a thief in the night," unexpectantly. In verse 3, Paul described the political conditions of that them. Peace and security will be the prevailing world view. Why is this? Daniel described this time:

> [24] Seventy weeks are determined on your people and on your holy city, to finish the transgression, and to make an end of sins, and to make reconciliation for iniquity, and to bring in everlasting righteousness, and to seal up the vision and prophecy, and to anoint the most Holy. [25] Know therefore and understand, that from the going forth of the commandment to restore and to build Jerusalem to the Messiah the Prince will be seven weeks, and threescore and two weeks: the street will be built again, and the wall, even in troublous times. [26] And after threescore and two weeks will Messiah be cut off, but not for himself: and the people of the prince that will come will destroy the city and the sanctuary; and the end thereof will be with a flood, and to the end of the war desolations are determined. [27] And he will confirm the covenant with many for one week: and in the midst of the week he will cause the sacrifice and the oblation to cease, and for the overspreading of abominations he will make it desolate, even until the consummation, and that determined will be poured on the desolate (Daniel 9.24-27).

The total period noted is seventy weeks, 490 years. Until the day of the Lord, 483 years have passed and seven remain. The day of the Lord, the Tribulation, will be initiated by the Beast signing a Middle East peace treaty. He will establish peace and the world will rejoice. It will be hailed as one of the world's greatest achievements and people with think a golden age is at hand. But such optimism is fleeting. After three and a half years, the Beast will stop the Jewish sacrifices in the rebuilt Temple and declare that he is God.

The Day of the Lord is the great subject of the prophets and constitutes Jewish theology. This Day includes two great themes: God's wrathful judgment on the earth and God's kingdom on earth when the Lord will fulfill all His covenant promises to Israel. Most often, however, the phrase refers to His wrath. Hundreds of verses describe this time in the Old Testament and it was a principal subject Jesus taught in His earthly ministry as well as what James, Peter, John, and Jude wrote in their letters. The following are examples of the Day of the Lord from the prophets:

> For the day of the LORD of hosts will be on everyone that is proud and lofty, and on everyone that is lifted up; and he will be brought low (Isaiah 2.12).

> 6 Howl! For the day of the LORD is at hand; it will come as a destruction from the Almighty. 7 Therefore will all hands be faint, and every man's heart will melt (Isaiah 13.6-7).

> For this is the day of the Lord GOD of hosts, a day of vengeance, that he may avenge him of his adversaries: and the sword will devour, and it will be satiate and made drunk with their blood: for the Lord GOD of hosts has a sacrifice in the north country by the river Euphrates (Jeremiah 46.10).

> 1 The word of the LORD came again to me, saying, 2 Son of man, prophesy and say, Thus says the Lord GOD; Howl, Woe to the day! 3 For the day is near, even the day of the LORD is near, a cloudy day; it will be the time of the heathen (Ezekiel 30.1-3).

> Alas for the day! For the day of the Lord is at hand, and as a destruction from the Almighty will it come (Joel 1.15).

> 1 Blow the trumpet in Zion, and sound an alarm in my holy mountain: let all the inhabitants of the land tremble: for the day of the LORD comes, for it is near at hand; 2 A day of darkness and of gloominess, a day of clouds and of thick darkness, as the

> morning spread on the mountains: a great people and a strong; there has not been ever the like, neither will be any more after it, even to the years of many generations (Joel 2.1-2).
>
> [14] The great day of the LORD is near, it is near, and hastens greatly, even the voice of the day of the LORD: the mighty man will cry there bitterly. [15] That day is a day of wrath, a day of trouble and distress, a day of wasteness and desolation, a day of darkness and gloominess, a day of clouds and thick darkness, [16] A day of the trumpet and alarm against the fenced cities, and against the high towers. [17] And I will bring distress on men, that they will walk like blind men, because they have sinned against the LORD: and their blood will be poured out as dust, and their flesh as the dung. [18] Neither their silver nor their gold will be able to deliver them in the day of the LORD's wrath; but the whole land will be devoured by the fire of his jealousy: for he will make even a speedy riddance of all them that dwell in the land (Zephaniah 1.14-18).

Paul described the world's attitude when Tribulation events begin (verse 3). He declared, "when they should say, Peace and security, then, sudden destruction comes on them." The world's political leaders and media proclaim a narrative of peace and safety—a lie. Instead, destruction falls.

What is most striking and informative about verses 3-11 is the contrast of the pronouns, "they" and "them" versus "you," "we," and "us"—more proof of the Pre-Tribulation Rapture. Thus, Paul wrote in verse 3, "for when they should say, Peace and security," "they" are unbelievers. Destruction falls on "them." These pains are likened to a woman's birth pains. It is impossible for them to escape—Paul used the double negative οὐ μὴ with the subjunctive, the strongest negation. After the Lord removes His Church, the die is cast. Judgment is coming.

Verse 4 contrasts unbelievers and members of the Church, the body of Christ, denoted as "But you, brethren." Paul declared the Thessalonians were "not in darkness, so the day should overtake you as a thief." The expression "the day" is the day of the Lord, noted in verse 2. Later, he wrote the Colossians similarly:

> [12] thanking the Father, the One who qualified us for the share of the saints' inheritance in the light, [13] who rescued us from the power of the darkness and transferred *us* into the kingdom of His beloved Son, [14] in whom we have the redemption through His blood, the forgiveness of the sins (Colossians 1.12-14).

This passage is understood by most as a statement about our salvation from sin and death. This is true, but it is likely more. Paul used the same verb ῥύομαι, "rescue" in the phrase, "who rescued us from the power of the darkness," ὃς ἐρρύσατο ἡμᾶς ἐκ τῆς ἐξουσίας τοῦ σκότους (verse 13), used in 1 Thessalonians 1.10, where he wrote "Jesus, the One who rescues us from the coming wrath," Ἰησοῦν τὸν ῥυόμενον ἡμᾶς ἀπὸ τῆς ὀργῆς τῆς ἐρχομένης. The expression, "the power of the darkness" describes the world system under Satan's control, his theater of deceit in contrast to Christ's kingdom of truth and light. This passage and 1 Thessalonians 1.10 are parallel. Christ has rescued us from the power of the darkness and transferred us into the kingdom of His beloved Son *positionally* for Paul wrote the Ephesians that God has blessed us with every spiritual blessing in the heavenlies in Christ (Ephesians 1.3) and "raised and seated *us* together in the heavenlies in Christ Jesus (Ephesians 2.6). The aorist verbs ἐρρύσατο, "rescued," and μετέστησεν, "transferred" are also proleptic, futuristic, describing Christ's rescue and transfer of believers at the Rapture. The verb μεθίστημι is formed by the preposition μετά and the verb ἵστημι, "stand" and means a change of position from one place to another, a removal, a transfer (cf. Luke 16.4; Acts 13.22, 19.26; 1 Corinthians 13.2; Colossians 1.13). The "power of the darkness" will reach its zenith in the Tribulation. Christ will rescue believers who are alive from it before it begins.

Paul expected the Rapture to occur in his lifetime and expected to experience a bodily removal from "the power of the darkness into the kingdom of His dear Son." Positionally, we are "in Christ." One day, we will be with Him bodily, seeing Him face to face.

Proleptic aorists are not common but Paul used them to denote God's faithfulness and integrity—the event is so certain it is expressed as past (cf. Ephesians 2.6). Another example of a proleptic aorist is Romans 8.30, "And whom He declared righteous, these He also glorified." The verbs "declared righteous," ἐδικαίωσεν, and "glorified," ἐδόξασεν, are aorists. Justification occurs the moment one believes Paul's gospel, a past act. Glorification, however, is future (proleptic aorist) but from Paul's perspective, and from God's perspective, it has occurred already for it is certain—God is faithful. In the same sense, God's removal of believers from earth before the Tribulation is described as a past event though it is future.

Paul continued this description of the Thessalonian believers in verse 5 as "sons of light and sons of day" (cf. Philippians 2.15) and stated, "we are not of night or of darkness." He further contrasted believers of his gospel and unbelievers with an allusion of sleep and night in verses 6-7. He declared, "we should not sleep as the others." "The others" are unbelievers but "we (believers) should stay alert and be sober." In verse 7, he wrote that sleepers sleep at night.

Night is the realm of darkness. Those asleep, in darkness, live in a false reality, a world of illusion shaped by Satan. Paul went on to say, "drunkards get drunk at night." Drunkenness is a condition of illusion and impaired control. Under such condition, one who is drunk does things he would not do if sober, another picture of Satan's illusionary fantasy world.

The Bible reveals Satan's character and strategy early in Genesis when he conversed with the woman. He told her the fruit of the forbidden tree would not cause death as God said, but would make her like a god, knowing good and evil. This was a lie. Everything that Satan promises is twisted truth and illusion.

Religions such as Hinduism and Buddhism recognize a world of illusion, *maya*, where things are not what they seem. Such perception is correct and beneficial. But on the other hand, these religions themselves are part of Satan's "magic show." Satan is the grandmaster of illusion and deceives most of humanity by many methods and devices. Most fall prey to them, which is why the Lord declared of His salvation "few are the ones who find it" (Matthew 7.13-14). Few choose to exit the illusion and come to the truth.

Sadly, however, even after coming to know Christ and His salvation, the vast majority of believers continue to live in a false reality, guided by tradition rather than the Scriptures. Should one doubt this, the proof is the thousands of denominations that exist. If believers understood and correctly followed the Scriptures, we would expect far greater unity with a small number of denominations than exist in Christendom. Satan has succeeded in using tradition and confusing the Scriptures to blind believers about God's plan and especially Paul's ministry and secrets.

Most believers are under the misconception that Paul was an appendage to the Twelve, a thirteen apostle, rather than the Lord's special, handpicked apostle who began the Church, the body of Christ, and reveal all Church doctrine. Unless one understands Paul's unique apostleship and that he revealed truths God had kept hidden, one cannot understand Church theology.

Paul continued in verse 8, stating that "we," believers, are of the day and should be sober, by "putting on *the* breastplate of faith and love, and *the* helmet—*the* hope of salvation." Paul saw many Roman soldiers and how they were equipped and protected for battle. Faith and love are the Christian's breastplate, protecting the heart. The hope of salvation is the believer's helmet, protecting the head. This is our armor. Throughout Paul's letters the trinity of faith, hope, and love occur and are most noteworthy in his letter to the Corinthians where he wrote that sign gifts of prophecy, knowledge, and languages would cease but faith, hope, and love would continue, the greatest of these being love (1 Corinthians 13.13).

Faith and love should be the operational characteristics of a believer's life. Faith is believing God and one who believes God, obeys God. Thus, love's source is faith. In one of the Lord's encounters with the Pharisees, one of them asked Him what was the great commandment (hoping to entrap Him). They expected Him to quote from the Decalogue. Instead, the Lord replied, "You will love *the* Lord your God with all your heart, and with all your soul, and with all your mind" (Matthew 22.37; cf. Deuteronomy 6.5). He continued, quoting Leviticus 19.18, "Now *the* second *is* like it, You will love your neighbor as yourself. On these two commandments hang the whole Law and the Prophets" (Matthew 22.39-40). The love of God is the source of good. If one loves God, one will also love his fellow man.

The hope of salvation should be firmly fixed in every believer's mind—it is his destiny. The Scriptural meaning of "hope" is anticipation and expectation, an assurance, not a "hope so." Salvation is assured for it rests on God's faithfulness.

---

9 Because the God did not appoint us for wrath but for obtaining salvation through our Lord Jesus Christ,
10 the One who died for us, so that whether we should watch or should sleep we should live together with Him.
11 Therefore, encourage one another and edify one another, even as you are also doing.

Comment:

Verses 9-11: In verses 9-11, Paul concluded this section, reiterating what he had declared before that believers of his gospel would not experience God's wrath. He wrote, "the God did not appoint us for wrath but for obtaining salvation through our Lord Jesus Christ." Most of the time when Paul used the noun ὀργή, "wrath," he used it for the Tribulation, the Day of the Lord, as here and earlier in 1 Thessalonians 1.10 and 2.16.

Notice the pronoun "us" in contrast to "they," "them," "others." Again, "us" means members of the Church, the body of Christ. The verb translated "appoint" is τίθημι, and means to "set" or "place" something into a position. God has not put members of the Church in a position for wrath but has destined us "for obtaining salvation through our Lord Jesus Christ."

What is this salvation? Paul did not mean salvation from sin and death. A believer obtains this the moment he believes. This salvation is deliverance from God's wrath, the Tribulation. Paul's language repeats 1 Thessalonians 1.10 where he stated, "the One who rescues us from the coming wrath." He would write similarly to the Romans:

> Much more, therefore, since we were now declared righteous by His blood, we will be saved from the wrath through Him (Romans 5.9)

This future salvation also cannot be salvation from sin and death for the first part of the verse states, "we were now declared righteous by His blood." Our salvation from sin and death and His righteousness are present possessions, not future hopes. All who have believed Paul's gospel and have become members of the Church need not fear the Tribulation. If we are alive at that time, Christ will take us from earth before it begins. Paul's "we" indicated he thought he would experience it.

While some have proposed a mid-tribulation or a post-tribulation Rapture, such views are without Scriptural support. Those who teach such views do not understand the difference between God's prophetic program for Israel and the Gentiles (nations) and

God's program of the Church, the body of Christ. If one mixes the Scriptures which deal with Israel and the nations with those which concern with the Church, error and confusion is the result.

In verse 10, Paul identified Christ as "the One who died for us," his gospel. He went on to reiterate the two possibilities for us as members of the Church: watching, awaiting Christ's return to rescue us from the Tribulation or sleep, i.e., death. Whatever category we are in (the vast majority are those who have or will die in Christ), we will live with Christ. Christ is our destiny: we in Him and He in us.

Because of this, Paul commanded (verse 11), "encourage one another," παρακαλεῖτε ἀλλήλους, the same phrase he used in 1 Thessalonians 4.18. He also commanded the Thessalonians to οἰκοδομεῖτε εἷς τὸν ἕνα "edify one another." Literally, the text εἷς τὸν ἕνα reads "one the one" or "one the other," an idiom with the same sense as ἀλλήλους. Paul noted they were building up one another and encouraged them to continue. As noted in 1 Thessalonians 4.18, believers who do not encourage one another with the Pre-Tribulation Rapture disobey Christ.

Christian Living

12 Now we ask you, brethren, to appreciate those who labor among you, and lead you in the Lord, and admonish you,
13 and to esteem them most highly in love because of their work. Be at peace among yourselves.
14 Now we urge you brethren, admonish the insubordinate, encourage the disheartened, support the weak, be patient to everyone.
15 See that no one should repay evil for evil to anyone, but always pursue the good for one another and for everyone.
16 Rejoice always.
17 Pray unceasingly.
18 Give thanks in everything. For this *is the* will of God in Christ Jesus for you.
19 Do not quench the Spirit.
20 Do not despise prophecies.

21 But examine all things. Hold firmly to the good.
22 Keep away from every appearance of evil.

Comment:

Verses 12-22: This series of terse commands by Paul should characterize our lives as believers.

In verses 12-13, Paul urged believers to appreciate those who worked, led, and admonished them in the Lord. They were to esteem highly such ministers in love. It is appropriate for believers to recognize, honor, and love those who faithfully serve and teach—those who give believers an understanding of the Scriptures and encourage them in the Christian life.

Paul also told them to live in peace. Every group is composed of people with various personalities and interests. Inevitably, we may not like some believers. We may find them irritating and annoying. We are not commanded to *like* them; we are commanded to *love* them. *Liking* a person is emotional. The Greek verb for the love we are commanded to have is ἀγαπάω (noun ἀγάπη), which denotes a mental, willful attitude—desiring another's good, wanting the best for them (cf. Matthew 5.43-44, 22.37, 39). Paul described this love to the Corinthians:

> 4 The love [ἀγάπη] is patient, is kind. The love [ἀγάπη] does not envy. The love [ἀγάπη] is not boastful, not arrogant. 5 It is not rude, it is not self-serving, is not easily provoked, does not keep an account of the wrong. 6 It does not rejoice at the unrighteousness, but rejoices in the truth. 7 It bears all things, believes all things, hopes all things, endures all things. 8 The love [ἀγάπη] never fails (1 Corinthians 13.4-8a).

The Greek verb for liking another, emotional affection or love is φιλέω (noun φιλία). It is not commanded. Despite differences, since members of the Church have the bond of faith and are part of Christ's body, we should strive for peace as much as possible despite differences and disagreements.

After urging peace, Paul exhorted them to admonish the insubordinate, encourage the disheartened, support the weak, and be patient to everyone (verses 14-15). Problems exist among believers because we still have a fallen nature and remain in a fallen world with tragedy, disappointments, stress, illness, and death. Every group of believers has those who are pushy, argumentative, lazy, unhappy, and weak. Such persons are to be encouraged or corrected as appropriate.

Despite problems, Paul counseled that no one should repay evil with evil but should pursue good for one another and everyone (verse 15). He spoke from experience for he endured more abuse, betrayal, and suffering than almost anyone. Despite this, he exemplified love, joy, thanksgiving, and patience.

Our current status is living in a fallen world but as members of the Church, the body of Christ, we have a glorious destiny: children of God, heirs of God, joint-heirs with Christ (Romans 8.17). We will govern with Christ and rule angels (1 Corinthians 6.2-3). We will have immortal, glorious bodies and live forever in God's presence.

With these things in mind, Paul encouraged the Thessalonians to "Rejoice always" (verse 16). Joy and rejoicing characterized Paul's ministry and life, despite his sufferings. He commanded us to "Pray unceasingly" (verse 17). Prayer was Paul's constant practice. One can pray anywhere, anytime. Prayer keeps us close to the Lord, in constant communication with Him.

In verse 18, Paul commanded us to "Give thanks in everything." The secret to joy is thankfulness. A thankful believer is a joyful believer. Paul wrote that this was God's will in Christ for us.

By God's indwelling Spirit we partake in the infinite and eternal. We are not to "quench the Spirit" (verse

19) for the living God, who created everything and sustains all life lives in every member of the Church. This should encourage us to live pleasing to Him.

The verb translated "quench," σβέννυμι, is used seven other times in the New Testament for extinguishing fire (Matthew 12.20, 25.8; Mark 9.44, 46, 48; Ephesians 6.16; Hebrews 11.34). Angels are spirits and spirits are described as fire (Hebrews 1.7). God is Spirit and revealed as fire throughout the Bible—the burning bush Moses saw (Exodus 3.2), the pillar of fire that gave Israel light during the night (Exodus 13.21-22), the fire on the Tabernacle (Numbers 9.15-16), the fire Ezekiel saw in his vision (Ezekiel 1.4), the effect of Christ's presence when the men walked with Him to Emmaus (Luke 24.32), etc. Fire exhibits power and activity. We are not to extinguish God's indwelling presence and power by sin.

In verse 20, Paul commanded believers not to despise prophecies. Prophecy does not concern the Church *per se* for prophecy involves God's program for Israel and the nations (Gentiles). Since this is so, perhaps some of the Thessalonians were disregarding and despising it. God has given us the entire Scripture for edification. Even though all Scripture is not to the Church, all is for us. Paul also wrote all Scripture is God-breathed (θεόπνευστος) and profitable (2 Timothy 3.16-17). We are to study, understand, and gain instruction from the entire Bible (cf. Romans 15.4; 1 Corinthians 10.11).

In verse 21, Paul commanded us to "examine all things." As members of the Church, we should not be naïve or gullible. The verb translated "examine" is δοκιμάζω, a verb used for testing metals or other items to determine genuineness. In His earthly ministry, Jesus counseled His disciples to be "wise as serpents" (Matthew 10.16). Paul wrote the Romans similarly:

> For your obedience reached all. Therefore, I am glad for you. But I want you to be wise for the good but blameless for the evil (Romans 16.19).

He wrote the Corinthians:

> Brethren, do not be children in your thinking. But be children in the evil. Be grownups in your thinking (1 Corinthians 14.20).

To the Ephesians he declared:

> Therefore, pay careful attention how you walk, not as unwise, but as wise (Ephesians 5.15).

Also in verse 21, Paul instructed us to "hold firmly" to the good (verse 21). The verb translated "hold firmly," κατέχω, means to hold fast or possess. What should be possessed is "the good," τὸ καλὸν. The noun καλός denotes what is beautiful, excellent, honorable, harmonious, complete. With the article, "the good," it denotes things God has given believers. In the LXX, καλός is first found in Genesis 1.4, "And God saw the light, that it was good (καλόν)" and throughout God's pronouncements of the six days. It also was used to describe the tree of knowledge of good and evil (καλοῦ καὶ πονηροῦ).

Final Blessings

23 Now may the God of the peace Himself sanctify you completely. And may your whole spirit, and soul, and body be preserved blameless at the coming of our Lord Jesus Christ.
24 The One who calls you is faithful, who will also do *it*.
25 Brethren, pray for us.
26 Greet all the brethren with *a* holy kiss.
27 I charge you *by* the Lord that this letter be read to all the holy[1] brethren.
28 The grace of our Lord Jesus Christ *be* with you! Amen.

Comment:

Verses 23-28: The God of the Bible is the God of peace (verse 23). He alone brings peace to the human heart, hearts enslaved to sin and death as children of

---

[1] Some manuscripts do not have "the holy," τοῖς ἁγίοις.

Adam, removed from God's paradise. God will sanctify the believer completely and this work begins the moment one believes the gospel. It is completed with our resurrection. Until then, sanctification is a daily process. The verb rendered "sanctify," ἁγιάζω, (verse 23) means "set apart." Paul used it in the following verses: Romans 15.16; 1 Corinthians 1.2, 6.11, 7.14; Ephesians 5.26; 1 Thessalonians 5.23; 1 Timothy 4.5; 2 Timothy 2.21; Hebrews 2.11, 9.13, 10.10, 14, 29, 13.12. God has "set apart" all who have put their trust in the Lord Jesus Christ, who are being conformed into the image of Christ (Romans 8.29), who is the image of God (2 Corinthians 4.4).

Paul wished our whole "spirit, and soul, and body" (cf. Hebrews 4.12) to be preserved blameless at the coming our Lord Jesus Christ. We are tripartite beings, incomplete without body, soul, and spirit. Spirit and soul are our immaterial parts and our body is our material part, housing the immaterial. Judaism and Christianity know nothing of souls and spirits without bodies. While death separates spirit and soul from the body, this condition is temporary. Both believers and unbelievers have body, soul, and spirit for eternity.

Those who have placed their trust in the God of the Bible are part of the "resurrection of life" (John 5.29). Some have received resurrection bodies as "firstfruits" (1 Corinthians 15.20; Matthew 27.52-53). Members of the Church will receive them at the Rapture. Those left will receive them at the end of the Tribulation (Daniel 12.11-13; Revelation 20.4-5).

Unbelievers are also resurrected, their souls and spirits reunited with their bodies at the end of the Millennium. They will stand bodily before Christ to be judged according to their works. Christ will judge and send them to the Lake of the Fire for eternity for they chose to reject His love and salvation (Revelation 20.11-14).

The Lord conquered death by His resurrection. Those who trust Him share in this victory. His victory is our victory. The "coming of our Lord Jesus Christ" in verse 23 is the Pre-Tribulation Rapture, not His

Second Advent and the Rapture is the Church's "blessed hope" (Titus 2.13).

Paul reminded believers God is faithful (verse 24). God appears to move slowly for we experience time serially and our mortal life is brief. But from God's perspective, the ages are a blink of the eye (2 Peter 3.8). Despite our perception, God will complete everything He has promised.

Paul requested they pray for him (verse 25) and greet fellow believers with a holy kiss (verse 26). We should pray for all who know the Lord and warmly welcome fellow believers.

Under the Lord's authority, Paul commanded this letter be read to all believers (verse 27). The verb translated "charge," ὁρκίζω, means to place under an oath. This language makes 1 Thessalonians unique among all books in the Bible. No other book has such language that it must be read. The closest comparative language is Colossians 4.16.

Does one hear this taught from the pulpit? Likely not in the vast majority of churches. Why did Paul place believers under an oath to read 1 Thessalonians? Its main subject is the Pre-Tribulational Rapture. Such strong language reveals how important God views this doctrine for His Church. Paul commanded believers twice in the letter to encourage one another with it (1 Thessalonians 4.18, 5.9-11). Obedient believers will read 1 Thessalonians, believing and encouraging one another with the Pre-Tribulation Rapture.

As the apostle of grace, Paul closed the letter with his customary statement of grace, "The grace of our Lord Jesus Christ *be* with you! Amen." Such a grace statement closes all of Paul's letters to the Church (Romans 16.24; 1 Corinthians 16.23; 2 Corinthians 13.14; Galatians 6.18; Ephesians 6.24; Philippians 4.23; Colossians 3.18; 1 Thessalonians 5.28; 2 Thessalonians 3.18; 1 Timothy 6.21; 2 Timothy 4.22; Titus 3.15; Philemon 1.25) as well as his letter to the Jews (Hebrews 11.25).

Introduction to 2 Thessalonians

Paul's second letter to the Thessalonians followed shortly after his first, probably in 52 or 53 A.D., again from Corinth.

He wrote of his suffering (1 Thessalonians 2.1-2), as well as theirs in 1 Thessalonians:

> [6] And you became imitators of us, even of the Lord, for you received the word in much affliction, with *the* joy of *the* Holy Spirit, [7] so you became *an* example to all the believers in Macedonia and Achaia (1 Thessalonians 1.6-7).
>
> For you became imitators, brethren, of the congregations of the God that are in Judea in Christ Jesus. For you also suffered the same things as they from your own countrymen, even as they from the Jews (1 Thessalonians 2.14).

Concerned about the Thessalonians' well-being, Paul tried to visit them several times but was hindered by Satan. Despite this deterrence, he was able to send Timothy to check on them, who thankfully returned with a good report (1 Thessalonians 3).

More persecutions had occurred (2 Thessalonians 1.4-7) and in addition, a new threat emerged—false teachers declared (apparently through a forged letter from Paul) that the Thessalonians' troubles indicated they were in the Tribulation, the Day of the Lord (2 Thessalonians 2.2).

Such teaching was greatly disturbing, for right after they believed Paul's gospel, Paul taught them that members of Christ's body, the Church, would *not* experience the Tribulation. He had instructed them the Rapture must come before the Day of the Lord and that only after the Lord rescued the Church would the man of the sin, the son of the destruction, the Beast, appear.

This was the context of Paul's second letter. The main teaching, as 1 Thessalonians, is the Pre-Tribulation Rapture. Paul also provided prophetic information, rare for him, about the appearance of the "man of the lawlessness," the Beast of John's Revelation. He did this to give the Thessalonians a fuller understanding of end-time events and to assure them the Tribulation and the Beast's appearance could not come until the Lord removed His Church: He would indeed rescue them. In the meantime, they were to stand firmly in the faith, endure persecutions, and disassociate from those who taught contrary to Paul.

2 Thessalonians

2 Thessalonians 1

Greeting and Thanksgiving from Paul, Silas, and Timothy

1 Paul, and Silvanus, and Timothy to the church of *the*
Thessalonians in God our Father, and the Lord Jesus
Christ.
2 Grace to you and peace from God our Father and the
Lord Jesus Christ.
3 We ought always to thank the God for you, brethren,
as it is right, because your faith is greatly increasing
and the love of every one of you is abounding to one
another
4 so that we ourselves boast about you in the churches
of the God about your endurance and faith in all your
persecutions and in the afflictions that you are
enduring.

Comment:

Verses 1-4: Like 1 Thessalonians, Paul gave his personal greeting along with Silvanus (Silas), and Timothy addressing "the church of the Thessalonians in God our Father, and the Lord Jesus Christ" (verse 1). As in the first letter, he greeted them with what became his signature "grace and peace" salutation (verse 2).

In verse 3, he declared they should always thank God for the Thessalonians—this was right—for their faith was greatly increasing and their love for one another abounding. The Thessalonians were a model church. Unlike the Corinthians and Galatians, Paul had no words of correction for them, only exhortation and encouragement.

Paul declared the Thessalonians were so excellent that he boasted to other churches of their endurance and faith in the persecutions and troubles they were enduring (verse 4). Their example should encourage every church and believer. No matter what difficulties arise, God is in charge. We may not understand what or why something happens but we must never forget God is faithful. Paul wrote that all things work together for good for those who love God (Romans 8.28). One day God will reveal everything.

Christ's Rescue of His Church and Vengeance on Unbelievers

5 *This is* evidence of the righteous judgment of the God so you might be deemed worthy of the kingdom of the God for which you suffer.
6 For *it is* right for God to repay those who afflict you with tribulation,
7 and to you who are being afflicted, *to give* rest with us in the revelation of the Lord Jesus from heaven with His powerful angels,
8 by inflicting vengeance with flaming fire on those who do not know God and on those who do not obey the gospel of our Lord Jesus Christ,
9 who will pay the penalty of eternal ruin away from the face of the Lord and from the glory of His strength,
10 when He should come to be glorified by His saints and to be marveled at on that day by all who believed, because our testimony to you was believed.

Comment:

Verses 5-10: The main thought in this section is one of contrast. God will reveal His justice by punishing those persecuting the Thessalonians in the Tribulation but give the Thessalonians "rest" from that judgment. The sufferings the Thessalonians were presently experiencing showed they were "in the fight" between good and evil and testified their worthiness to live in God's kingdom (verse 5). In this vein, Paul would write Timothy, "And so, all who want to live godly in Christ Jesus will be persecuted" (2 Timothy 3.12).

The chief problem 2 Thessalonians reveals was the claim by false teachers that the afflictions the Thessalonians were experiencing indicated they were in the Tribulation. Paul wrote 2 Thessalonians to combat this assertion and reinforce what he wrote in 1 Thessalonians—Christ would rescue them, take them from the earth, before it began.

Some have seen a challenge to the Pre-Tribulation Rapture in verse 7, which states God would give the Thessalonians "rest" from persecutions "in the revelation of the Lord Jesus from heaven with His powerful angels," ἐν τῇ ἀποκαλύψει τοῦ κυρίου Ἰησοῦ ἀπ' οὐρανοῦ μετ' ἀγγέλων δυνάμεως αὐτοῦ. Understanding the passage requires answering the following:

1. What is the "tribulation" in verse 6?
2. What does "rest" mean in verse 7?
3. When does "rest" of verse 7 begin?
4. What is the revelation of Christ from heaven with His angels?

Before addressing these questions, a couple key principles of interpretation must be understood. The first is the principle of "reading from" a text, exegesis, ἐξήγησις, as opposed to "reading into" a text, eisegesis, εἰσήγησις. The other is comparing Scripture with Scripture. What may be unclear or difficult in one passage may be explained by another.

Paul taught the Pre-Tribulational Rapture throughout his letters. It is as solid a truth as his gospel. In his first letter to the Thessalonians, he wrote Christ would remove members of the Church from earth before the Tribulation. Would he now write the Thessalonians something different? No. Paul's main purpose in 2 Thessalonians was to strengthen what he wrote in his first letter—they would not undergo the Tribulation.

Paul declared it was right for God to repay the Thessalonians' persecutors with tribulation (verse 6). Since Paul thought the Lord would return for His Church in his lifetime and then complete His prophetic program, the "tribulation" of verse 6 is the Tribulation, the time of God's wrath, the Day of the Lord, Daniel's 70th week.

Paul was not alone in the view that the Tribulation would soon come. All the other apostles and writers, Peter, James, John, Jude, stated this. Peter's words on the day of Pentecost, when he quoted Joel's prophesy, included the advent of the Holy Spirit as well as the sun turning to darkness and the moon to blood, a prophecy of the Tribulation (Acts 2.19-20; cf. Joel 2.30-31). By the time Paul wrote the Thessalonians, twenty years had passed. They anticipated God would soon consummate His prophetic plan.

The divine "repayment" of those afflicting the Thessalonians was the Tribulation. This is clarified in verse 8 where Paul described God's vengeance in the Tribulation as "by inflicting vengeance with flaming fire on those who do not know God and on those who do not obey the gospel of our Lord Jesus Christ."

Verses 6 and 7 parallel and contrast one another. Paul stated in verse 6 that it was right for God to repay the Thessalonians' persecutors with tribulation (the Tribulation) and verse 7 states it was right for God to give the Thessalonians, "rest with us," with Paul, Silvanus, and Timothy "in the revelation of the Lord Jesus from heaven with all His powerful angels."

What did Paul mean by "rest," ἄνεσιν, in verse 7? The noun ἄνεσιν means "relief" (cf. 2 Corinthians 2.1, 7.5, 8:13) and is associated with the verb ἀνίημι, which means "loosening" or "slackening" something in tension, e.g., a bowstring. The "rest" is relief from persecution. This "rest" begins at the Rapture, Christ's rescue of living members of the Church before the Tribulation (Daniel's 70th week) begins.

Those who maintain this verse challenges the Pre-Tribulation Rapture assert this rest begins "in the revelation of the Lord Jesus from heaven, with His powerful angels," at His Second Advent. It is clear Paul meant Christ's Second Advent for he described it in verse 8 with "by inflicting vengeance with flaming fire on those who do not know God."

If "rest" is the Rapture, how can it be before the Tribulation if it does not begin until the Lord's Second Advent? An even more incisive question is that if this is true, in what sense could this be "rest?" If Paul meant the Thessalonians and himself had to experience the persecutions of the Tribulation until the Lord returned at its end at the Second Advent, how could he describe this as "rest?" How would their condition be different from their tormentors? How would such "comfort" allay the Thessalonians' fears?

The *only* reasonable explanation is that "rest" begins before Christ's Second Advent, at the Rapture, before the Tribulation and continues until Christ's return. Does this read into the text what is not there? Paul wrote that God would give rest in Christ's Second Advent. However, he did *not* write it would *begin* at Christ's Second Advent. The view that "rest" does not begin until Christ's Second Advent is based on assumption—a false assumption. How could this comfort the Thessalonians? If they and Paul must undergo the Tribulation along with their tormentors, how could this be "rest?" How could this accord with verse 6, "For *it is* right for God to repay those who afflict you with tribulation?" We must compare Scripture with Scripture to understand the text.

Paul taught and wrote the Thessalonians they would not experience the Tribulation (1 Thessalonians). In later letters, he continued to teach the Pre-Tribulation Rapture. How does all of this fit?

Revelation unveils that God brings many judgments in the Tribulation on humanity before Christ returns at the end. Paul mentioned none of these. If one were to read only verses 7-8, one might conclude no divine judgment occurs until Christ's return. Revelation reveals that Christ's return is the final judgment. It will be terrible—the slaughter at the battle of Armageddon will be massive (Revelation 14.18-20) and all earth's cities will collapse (Revelation 16.18-19). But

Revelation also reveals many judgments and woes occur before this in the seal, trumpet, and bowl judgments. Paul did not mention them. Thus, Christ's Second Advent summarizes all these judgments.

In 1 Thessalonians 1.10, Paul gave a brief statement about the Rapture. He followed it with details in 1 Thessalonians 4.13-5.11. The same pattern is present in 2 Thessalonians. Verses 7-8 briefly describe the Rapture and God's judgment. 2 Thessalonians 2.1-12 provide details.

Thus, verses 7-8 are a synecdoche, a figure of speech in which a part stands for the whole. The "rest" in verse 7 encompasses the period from the Rapture to Christ's Second Advent. The Lord's "repayment" (verse 6) of judgment in verses 6-8 includes all of God's judgments in the Tribulation. One does not "read into" the text that "rest" begins with the Pre-Tribulation Rapture and continues through the Tribulation any more than one "reads into" the text that Christ's return is the only judgment in the Tribulation. One Scripture expounds another under the hermeneutical principle of comparison. Verse 7 only challenges the Pre-Tribulation Rapture if one refuses to compare Scripture with Scripture and examine the context of Paul's exposition.

As noted above, God's judgment on evildoers, which Paul thought would include those persecuting the Thessalonians, is twofold. The first is His vengeance in the Tribulation "with flaming fire on those who do not know God and on those who do not obey the gospel of our Lord Jesus Christ" (verse 8).

The phrase "obey the gospel" expresses believing God's message of salvation. Paul wrote of the "obedience of faith," ὑπακοὴν πίστεως, in Romans 1.5 and 16.25, a genitive of apposition and means "obedience that is faith," or "obedience, namely, faith." To believe God is to obey God and obeying God is belief.

Disobedience of God apexes in the Tribulation, the Day of the Lord. Most of humanity will worship Satan. Most will commit the blasphemy of the Holy Spirit, the unforgivable sin, by taking the Beast's mark, sealing their eternal doom.

Verse 9 describes the second part of God's judgment of unbelievers, "the penalty of eternal ruin away from the face of the Lord and from the glory of His strength." The phrase "eternal ruin" is ὄλεθρον αἰώνιον. Paul is the only New Testament writer who used the noun ὄλεθρος, "ruin" (cf. 1 Corinthians 5.5; 1 Thessalonians 5.3; 2 Thessalonians 1.9; 1 Timothy 6.9). This noun is related to the verb ὀλλυμι and the compound form ἀπολλυμι. Most translations render ὄλεθρον αἰώνιον, "eternal destruction," but the better sense is "eternal ruin" or "eternal loss." For example, the Lord's parables of the lost sheep, coin, and son, use the verb ἀπολλυμι, describing the "lostness" of each (Luke 15.4, 6, 8-9, 17, 24, 32). No sound case can be made for the sense eternal annihilation or extinction.

Excursus: Eternal Punishment

The prophets had little to say about eternal punishment (Isaiah 66.22-24; Daniel 12.2). However, they wrote extensively of the Tribulation. In this vein, the above passage is only time Paul directly addressed eternal punishment. When he wrote about God's punishment, he meant the Tribulation, expressed with the word "wrath."[1] The same is true for Peter, James, John, and Jude (cf. Jude 1.7, 13; Revelation 14.9-11, 21.8). Why is this?

Perhaps because eternal punishment is so terrible only the Lord could speak about it at length. Indirectly, Paul wrote about eternal punishment with, "For the wages of the sin is death. But the gift of the God is eternal life in Christ Jesus our Lord," τὰ γὰρ ὀψώνια τῆς ἁμαρτίας θάνατος τὸ δὲ χάρισμα τοῦ θεοῦ ζωὴ αἰώνιος ἐν Χριστῷ Ἰησοῦ τῷ κυρίῳ ἡμῶν (Romans 6.23). "Death" is spiritual death, separation from God, in

---

[1] Eternal punishment is not God's wrath but penal justice.

contrast to "eternal life." Without Christ, death is our fate.

The Lord, like the prophets, spoke at length about the Tribulation but in contrast to the prophets, Paul, and the other writers, He also spoke extensively about eternal punishment: Hell and the Lake of Fire (cf. Matthew 5.22, 29-30, 7.13-14, 21-23, 8.10-12, 10.28, 13.29-30, 49-50, 18.8-9, 22.11-14, 23.13, 32-33, 24.50-51, 25.29-39, 40-46; Mark 3.28-29, 9.43-48; Luke 10.14-15, 12.4-5, 13.24-28, 16.22-28; John 5.28-29). Those who make a case against eternal punishment have Christ as their chief opponent.

Assaults against eternal punishment have come at various times throughout church history. Sometimes the subject becomes vogue, as it has been recently. Five basic objections exist to eternal punishment:

1. God wills all to be saved. Since He is sovereign, all will be saved.

Response: Paul declared God's wishes all to be saved. He wrote Timothy:

> 3 For this is right and acceptable before the God, our Savior, 4 who wants all men to be saved and come to the full knowledge of the truth (1 Timothy 2.4).

The verb translated "wants" is θέλω and means "want," "intend," "desire," "wish." Peter wrote:

> The Lord does not delay the promise, as some regard delay, but is patient to us, for He does not intend any to perish but for all to come to repentance (2 Peter 3.9).

Peter used the verb βούλομαι. While θέλω and βούλομαι overlap in meaning, the distinction between the verbs is usually that θέλω involves a general inclination or desire while βούλομαι is an act of the will after deliberation. An example is Matthew 1.19, "Now Joseph, her husband, since he was upright and did not wish (θέλω) to disgrace her, planned (βούλομαι) to send her away secretly." Ephesians 1.11

has the related nouns of these verbs, "according to the counsel (βουλή) of His will (θέλημα)."

Paul and Peter's statements reveal God's heart and will. He wishes all to be saved and intends none to perish. Because of this, He died for everyone's sins. While God has provided salvation for all, it does follow all will be saved. God's love for us and our being created in His image includes giving us free will. Salvation is available for all who *want* it. We must choose. God forces no one. He is no oppressor.

2. God reconciled man through the work of Christ, so all will be saved.

Response: God has reconciled the world to Himself (2 Corinthians 5.19). He did everything necessary from the divine standpoint for reconciliation. Salvation is a transaction: our sin and death for His righteousness and life. One must trust in what God has done. Paul wrote, "Be reconciled to God" (2 Corinthians 5.20). 1 Corinthians 15.22 reads, "For as all in the Adam die, so too all in the Christ will be made alive." Note that only those "in Christ" are made alive. Becoming "in Christ" results from a choice—trusting Christ. In our present age, trusting Christ means believing Paul's gospel, Christ for one's sins and rose from the dead (1 Corinthians 15.1-4). Apart from this, one remains outside Christ. Without faith, one cannot please God (Hebrews 11.6).

3. Words for eternal and destruction do not mean what they appear to mean.

Response: The objection concerns the words for "eternal," "forever," αἰών, αἰώνιος, and "destroy," ἀπόλλυμι. Objectors maintain the words αἰών and αἰώνιος mean "ages," long time spans, not "eternal." The noun αἰών can mean an age depending on context but the adjective αἰώνιος as used in the New Testament always means "eternal," "forever." In Romans 16.25, translators have rendered χρόνοις αἰωνίοις "long ages" but the words χρόνοις αἰωνίοις literally mean "in eternal times." One wonders why translators did this when in every other case αἰώνιος is rendered "eternal," "everlasting," "forever."

The next verse, Romans 16.26, confirms the "eternal" rendering. Paul stated, τοῦ αἰωνίου θεοῦ. If αἰώνιος means "an age" or "long time," did Paul mean God only exists for and an age? Was there a time when He did not exist and came into existence? In 1 Timothy 6.16, Paul wrote of Christ, ὁ μόνος ἔχων ἀθανασίαν, "the only One who has immortality," deathlessness. Paul concluded the verse, ᾧ τιμὴ καὶ κράτος αἰώνιον, "to whom be honor and might forever." Are we to assume Christ's honor and might exist only for an age? No. They are forever. Other passages, Luke 1.33; John 8.35; Romans 1.25 use the word αἰών. These verses indicate "forever," not "a long time." The following are all the uses of αἰώνιος in the New Testament: Matthew 18.8, 19.16, 29, 25.41, 46; Mark 3.29, 10.17, 30; Luke 10.25, 16.9, 18.18, 30; John 3.15-16, 36, 4.14, 36, 5.24, 39, 6.27, 40, 47, 54, 68, 10.28, 12.25, 50, 17.2-3; Acts 13.46, 48; Romans 2.7, 5.21, 6.22-23, 16.25-26; 2 Corinthians 4.17-18, 5.1; Galatians 6.8; 2 Thessalonians 1.9, 2.16; 1 Timothy 1.16, 6.12, 16, 19; 2 Timothy 1.9, 2.10; Titus 1.2, 3.7; Philemon 1.15; Hebrews 5.9, 6.2, 9.12, 14-15, 13.20; 1 Peter 5.10; 2 Peter 1.11; 1 John 1.2, 2.25, 3.15, 5.11, 13, 20; Jude 1.7, 21; Revelation 14.6. Finally, if punishment is not "eternal," neither is eternal life, for the same word, αἰώνιος, is used for both (e.g. Matthew 25.46).

The word rendered "destroy," ἀπόλλυμι, never means "annihilation" or "extinction." It means loss, ruin, or undoing. It can mean loss of life, death, but never loss of existence. Jesus said eternal punishment involves "the weeping and the grinding of the teeth," ὁ κλαυθμὸς καὶ ὁ βρυγμὸς τῶν ὀδόντων (Matthew 8.12, 22.13, 24.51, 25.30; Luke 13.28). One annihilated has no teeth to grind.

4. God's punishment is corrective, not punitive.

Response: Some argue divine punishment is probationary and corrective. But since "punishment" is linked with "eternal," κόλασιν αἰώνιον (Matthew 25.46; cf. Daniel 12.2; Matthew 25.41; Mark 9.44, 46, 48; Revelation 14.11), what is the sense of "eternal correction?" It is meaningless.

Jesus' story of Lazarus and the rich man in Luke 16.19-31 reveals an important truth. The rich man wished to be relieved from suffering and did not want his brothers to experience his fate. He wanted them warned so they might repent. But the rich man himself showed no inclination for repentance. Those in eternal punishment have sorrow (weeping and grinding of teeth) about their condition but will not repent. This is one reason the punishment must be eternal. No repentance exists for those in hell or those whom God will send to the Lake of the Fire. This is why C. S. Lewis wrote the gates of hell are locked on the inside. They are self-exiled; they continue to resist God—the manward side of eternal punishment.

On the Godward side, God will not allow those who have rejected His salvation and remain in rebellion to Him to live in His presence or in the presence of those who love Him. Throughout history God allows wheat and the tares (believers and unbelievers) to coexist. That environment ceases in eternity, in the new heavens and new earth. It would be an affront to God's holiness and impossibly cruel for God to let those antagonistic to Him to live forever among those who love Him. It would also be cruel to those who want nothing to do with Him to be in His presence. John was told in Revelation 22.11, "The one who is unrighteous, let him continue unrighteous. And the one who is filthy, let him remain filthy. And the one who is righteous, let him continue doing righteousness. And the one who is holy, let him remain holy." Of the New Jerusalem John wrote, "Now outside are the dogs, and the sorcerers, and the sexually immoral, and the murderers, and the idolaters, and everyone who loves and does falsehood (Revelation 22.15). Those "outside" are in the Lake of the Fire, outside the new heaven and the new earth.

God creates a new heaven and a new earth because everything in the original creation has been corrupted by sin. The new creation is fresh with no possibility of sin. As the great Tyndale wrote, "When God buildeth, He casteth all downe first. He is no patcher."

5. God is love and His character is inconsistent with consigning men to eternal punishment.

Response: God is love. God loves every person. His greatest demonstration of love was becoming man, suffering at the hands of the Jews and Romans, and bearing our sins and its penalty, death. Love requires freedom. Salvation demands freedom. It cannot be forced. God gave us wills to accept or reject Him. Eternal punishment is terrible and should terrify every person—hence Jesus' constant warnings. But for God to force His creatures to love and worship Him would be worse. He made us in His image (Genesis 1.26-27) with freedom to choose. God has given ample witness of Himself (John 1.9; Romans 1.19-20; Titus 2.11; Colossians 1.23; cf. Luke 16.31). Every person can accept His love and salvation or reject it. In *The Problem of Pain*, C. S. Lewis wrote, "If a game is played, it must be possible to lose it." We choose.

Arguments against eternal punishment are logically flaccid and without Scriptural support. The Scriptures cited against eternal punishment are twisted to mean something they do not. At best, they are wishful thinking. At worst, they are rebellion against God and defiance of His word. People choose to go to hell and the Lake of Fire by rejecting God's love and salvation. Those who so choose remain in rebellion to Him.

It is noteworthy that objectors to eternal punishment do not take on the Lord Himself and His statements about eternal punishment. They skirt His words, only declaring they do not mean what they appear. In the end, there will be no excuses. All will acknowledge God is just in His punishment. Every knee will bow to Christ—joyfully and gladly by those with eternal life, grudgingly and bitterly by those eternally condemned.

The Lord reveals the glory of His strength (verse 9) at His return. Satan will display immense power in the Tribulation. John wrote, "And they worshiped the Dragon because he gave the power to the Beast. And they worshiped the Beast, saying, Who is like the

Beast? Who can fight against it" (Revelation 13.4)? But the Lord's return in glory will reveal Satan's weakness. He is no match for the Lord of glory. He will throw the Beast and False Prophet into the Lake of the Fire forever and imprison Satan in the Abyss for a thousand years.

At the Lord's Second Advent (verse 10), He will "be glorified by His saints and be marveled at (θαυμάζω) on that day by all who believed." Saints of all ages and programs are included. In particular, Paul wrote of his readers, "because our testimony to you was believed." The expression "on that day" occurs at the end of the sentence in the Greek text for emphasis. "That day" is Christ's Second Advent. Members of the Church with all other believers will glorify Him at His Second Advent, His victory on earth when He defeats Satan as "the god of this age," ὁ θεὸς τοῦ αἰῶνος τούτου (2 Corinthians 4.4).

---

11 For which also we always pray for you, so our God might deem you worthy of the calling and might complete every desire of goodness and work of faith with power,
12 so that the name of our Lord Jesus Christ might be glorified in you and you in Him, according to the grace of our God and *the* Lord Jesus Christ.

Comment:

Verses 11-12: These verses close the section and emphasize Paul's attitude of constant prayer noted in 1 Thessalonians 1.2, 3, 3.13, 5.17. His words "for which also we always pray for you," εἰς ὃ καὶ προσευχόμεθα πάντοτε περὶ ὑμῶν, link what he wrote in verse 10 with what follows in verses 11 and 12, "so our God might deem you worthy of the calling, and might complete every desire of goodness and work of faith with power, so that the name of our Lord Jesus Christ might be glorified in you and you in Him, according to the grace of our God and the Lord Jesus Christ."

Paul's phrase "of the calling," τῆς κλήσεως, is the calling in which one becomes a member of the Church, the body of Christ, by believing the gospel (1 Corinthians 15.1-4; 1 Corinthians 12.12-27). As this new creation, the Church, we are to live worthy of this high calling. God's desire, for which Paul prayed, was for God to "complete every desire of goodness and work of faith with power." The phrase "work of faith," ἔργον πίστεως, is a genitive of result, work resulting from faith (cf. Ephesians 2.10). Believing God should motivate Christian work, for faith is obeying God. Such work is "with power" for works of faith are under the control of the Holy Spirit.

The result of this is "so that the name of our Lord Jesus Christ might be glorified in you and you in Him, according to the grace of our God and the Lord Jesus Christ" (verse 12). Christ's name being glorified in us results from obedience to Him, believing Him, under the control of the Holy Spirit.

This is how we share in God's glory as His children. Everything we have as believers is "according to the grace of our God and the Lord Jesus Christ." Our inheritance as fallen, children of Adam, is death and separation from God. God's goodness and grace brings us to Himself and makes us His heirs and joint-heirs of Christ. What a destiny!

2 Thessalonians 2

The Man of Sin Cannot Appear Before the Rapture

1 Now we ask you, brethren, concerning the coming of
our Lord Jesus Christ and of our gathering to Him,
2 that you might not be easily shaken in your mind or
be troubled, by neither spirit, or by word, or by *a* letter
as if through us, that the day of the Lord has arrived.
3 Do not let anyone deceive you in any way. For the
departure must come first and then the man of the
lawlessness should be revealed, the son of the
destruction,
4 the one who opposes and exalts himself above every
named god or object of worship, so that he will sit in
the Temple of the God and display himself: that he is
God.

Comment:

Verses 1-4: These verses begin the heart of Paul's letter, his primary reason for writing. He wished to assure them the afflictions they were experiencing did not mean they were in the Tribulation.

In verses 1-2, Paul asked the Thessalonians not to be troubled about the Lord's return and the Rapture. Do the expressions "the coming of our Lord Jesus Christ," τῆς παρουσίας τοῦ κυρίου ἡμῶν Ἰησοῦ Χριστοῦ, and "our gathering to Him," ἡμῶν ἐπισυναγωγῆς ἐπ' αὐτόν, describe one event or two? Paul used the noun παρουσία for both the Second Advent and the Rapture. In verse 8, the reference is clearly to the Lord's Second Advent. Here, in the context of what Paul is about to write, the reference to His coming is the Rapture. Thus, the "and," καί, of verse 1 has an ascensive use, "even" and connects the Lord's appearance with our gathering to Him, the Rapture.

The noun ἐπισυναγωγή, translated "gathering" is a contraction of the preposition ἐπί and noun συναγωγή (synagogue) and means a gathering or assembling. It is used one other time, in Hebrews 10.25, where Paul exhorted Jews who had believed the gospel of the kingdom not to forsake assembling together but to meet and encourage one another as they saw Christ's return drawing near.

As an aside, this exhortation is evidence Paul not only wrote Hebrews, but wrote it early, likely about 53 A.D., shortly after 1-2 Thessalonians. Most Bible scholars reject Paul's authorship of Hebrews and those who do accept it maintain he wrote the letter late, in the 60s. Both views are wrong.[1] The evidence for Pauline authorship of Hebrews is overwhelming and much stronger evidence exists for his writing the letter early in his ministry.

The "gathering to Him" (verse 1) describes what Paul wrote in 1 Thessalonians 4.13-18, that members of the Church who had died would be joined, gathered together, with those who were alive and meet the Lord in the air.

Paul wrote the Thessalonians not "to be shaken in your mind or troubled," σαλευθῆναι ὑμᾶς ἀπὸ τοῦ νοὸς μήτε θροεῖσθαι (verse 2). They were not to be upset "by neither spirit, or by word, or by *a* letter as if through us," διὰ πνεύματος μήτε διὰ λόγου μητὲ δι' ἐπιστολῆς ὡς δι' ἡμῶν. It appears the Thessalonians had received some communication allegedly from Paul that the Tribulation had come.

The KJV reads "the day of the Christ," ἡ ἡμέρα τοῦ Χριστοῦ, but overwhelming manuscript evidence is for "the day of the Lord." The expression, "the day of the Christ" includes the Rapture and Christ's judgment of works done by members of the Church. Paul used the phrase, "the day of the Christ" or "that day" in 1 Corinthians 1.8, 3.13, 5.5; 2 Corinthians 1.14; Philippians 1.6, 10, 2.16; 2 Timothy 1.18, 4.8.

Paul wrote the Corinthians about the judgment of works by members of the Church:

---

[1] This subject is dealt with at greater length in the author's books, *Paul: Apostle of Secrets* and *Understanding the Jewish Writings: An Examination of Hebrews, James, 1-2 Peter, 1-3 John, Jude, and Revelation.*

> [12] Now if anyone builds on this foundation gold, silver, precious stones, wood, hay, straw, [13] the work of each will become manifest, for the day will disclose *it*, for it is revealed by fire and fire will test the work of each, what kind it is. [14] If the work of anyone will remain that he built up, he will receive *a* reward. [15] If the work of anyone will be burned up, he will suffer loss. But he himself will be saved, so as through fire (1 Corinthians 3.12-15).

"The day of the Christ" is a day of rescue and a day of reward for members of the Church, in contrast to "the day of the Lord," a day of God's wrath, a day of doom.

Contextually, apart the manuscript evidence, it would make no sense for Paul to write them that "the day of Christ" had arrived. If that were the reading, it would mean the Thessalonians as well as Paul would have missed the Rapture. Paul's purpose in writing was to assure them their troubles was not "the day of the Lord," the Tribulation.

In verse 3, Paul commanded the Thessalonians not to let anyone deceive them in any way. To ensure this, he gave them a clear sign to foil deceit. He wrote, "the departure must come first and then the man of the sin should be revealed, the son of the destruction." What clear sign did Paul mean?

Most translations render the noun ἀποστασία as "apostasy" (NASB), "rebellion" (NIV, NET), "falling away" (KJV). This noun occurs twice in Scripture: 2 Thessalonians 2.3 and Acts 21.21. In the Acts passage, James questioned Paul about what they had heard: he was teaching Jews to "depart from" or "forsake" (ἀποστασία) Moses' teaching. In that passage, the noun ἀποστασία has no definite article and includes a qualifying prepositional phrase, "from Moses," ἀπὸ Μωσέως, a different grammatical construct from 2 Thessalonians 2.3, which has the definite article, ἡ ἀποστασία, and does not have a qualifying phrase. Paul wrote, ἡ ἀποστασία, indicating a specific event.

This event must occur before the Tribulation. What event would provide them with a clear sign?

"Apostasy" or "rebellion" provides no clear sign. It was pointless for Paul to give apostasy or rebellion as a "sign" of what must occur before the Tribulation and the appearance of the Beast for apostasy and rebellion *always exist*. The Thessalonians were experiencing these things from false teachers and by false doctrine. Warnings against false teachers and identifying false teaching fill the writings of Paul, James, Peter, John, and Jude. To allay the Thessalonians fears, Paul needed to give them a concrete sign to demonstrate they were not in the Tribulation. The Rapture is that sign—God's physical removal of His Church was the clearest sign possible. As long as they were on earth, the Tribulation had not come.

The verb associated with ἀποστασία is ἀφίστημι, and occurs fifteen times, only used by Paul and Luke (Luke 2.37, 4.13, 8.13, 13.27; Acts 5.37-38, 12.10, 15.38, 19.9, 22.29; 2 Corinthians 12.8; 1 Timothy 4.1, 6.5; 2 Timothy 2.19; Hebrews 3.12). In 2 Corinthians 12.8, 1 Timothy 6.5, and possibly 2 Timothy 2.19, Paul used the verb for physical removal.

Early English Bibles translated ἀποστασία as "departure" or "departing," e.g., Tyndale (1525), Coverdale (1535), Matthew (1537), Great (1539), Geneva (1560). Jerome's Latin Vulgate (c. 400 A.D.) translated ἀποστασία with "discessio," "departure." What these translators understood about end times is irrelevant. What is important is that they translated ἀποστασία as "departure."

The KJV translators broke from translating ἀποστασία as "departure" and rendered the noun "falling away," an alteration that connoted the idea of "apostasy" or "rebellion." This change influenced future translations which contributed to a flawed understanding of Paul's meaning.

Paul wrote ἡ ἀποστασία, "the x." The noun with the definite article, "the" indicated something clear and definite. If he meant a specific apostasy or rebellion, "the apostasy," it would surely denote mankind's greatest apostasy and rebellion—the world's worship of the Beast and accepting his mark. If it did not mean this particular rebellion, how would anyone recognize it, since apostasy and rebellion are always present?

But verse 3 states ἡ ἀποστασία comes *before* the Beast appears. If Paul meant the rebellion and apostasy of Tribulation, the verse makes *no sense*. Therefore, Paul had something else in mind.

Thus, the text reads, "the departure must come first and then the man of the sin should be revealed," ἔλθῃ ἡ ἀποστασία πρῶτον καὶ ἀποκαλυφθῇ ὁ ἄνθρωπος τῆς ἁμαρτίας. The adjective "first," πρῶτον, and the temporal use of καί (and) govern the order. Paul identified the person who appears after "the departure" with two phrases, "the man of the lawlessness," ὁ ἄνθρωπος τῆς ἀνομίας, and "the son of the destruction," ὁ υἱὸς τῆς ἀπωλείας. A variant reading exists with the first phrase. Many manuscripts read "the man of the sin," ὁ ἄνθρωπος τῆς ἁμαρτίας, rather than "the man of the lawlessness," ὁ ἄνθρωπος τῆς ἀνομίας. Both readings have broad manuscript support but τῆς ἀνομίας is likely the original reading due to the technical nature of Paul's argument.

Sadly, translations render ἀποστασία inaccurately in verse 3 and also fail to include the definite article in both phrases. The text does not read, "the man of lawlessness" and "the man of destruction" but "the man of the lawlessness" and "the man of the destruction." Inclusion of the definite article is highly significant as seen with ἡ ἀποστασία. The definite article with the nouns "lawlessness" and "destruction" denotes one who commits a specific kind of "lawlessness" and "destruction." The phrases identify this person as the Beast, Satan's representative.

Of the non-Pauline writers, only Matthew and John used the noun ἀνομία, "lawlessness." In Matthew and John, the definite article with the noun has a technical sense: the lawlessness practiced in the Tribulation:

worship of the Beast and taking his mark. When the Lord spoke about the Tribulation, He used the definite article with "lawlessness." Consider these verses:

> And then I will declare to them, I never knew you! Depart from Me you who produce the lawlessness (τὴν ἀνομίαν) (Matthew 7.23).

> The Son of the Man will send out His angels and they will gather from His kingdom all the offenders and those who practice the lawlessness (τὴν ἀνομίαν) (Matthew 13.41).

> And because the lawlessness (τὴν ἀνομίαν) becomes multiplied, the love of the many will grow cold (Matthew 24.12).

When the Lord meant lawlessness in general, He did not include the definite article:

> So also, outwardly you appear righteous to mankind. But inwardly, you are full of hypocrisy and lawlessness (ἀνομίας) (Matthew 23.28).

John used ἀνομία once, with the definite article. He wrote in 1 John 3.4:

> Everyone who commits the sin (τὴν ἁμαρτίαν) also commits the lawlessness (τὴν ἀνομίαν). So, the sin (ἡ ἁμαρτία) is the lawlessness (ἡ ἀνομία).

John wrote that "the sin," ἡ ἁμαρτία, is "the lawlessness," ἡ ἀνομία. Both nouns, "sin" and "lawlessness," have the definite article. What is "the sin?" The definite article with the noun denotes a specific sin, a specific act of lawlessness. John was writing about the unforgivable sin, the lawlessness that is the blasphemy of the Holy Spirit, the one sin Jesus declared would never be forgiven. He warned about committing this sin in His earthly ministry:

> And everyone who will say *a* word against the Son of the Man, it will be forgiven him. But the one who blasphemed the Holy

> Spirit, it will not be forgiven (Luke 12.10; cf. Matthew 12.31-32; Mark 3.28-29).

John identified this sin in Revelation:

> 9 And another angel, a third, followed them, who said in a loud voice, If anyone worships the Beast and his image and accepts the mark on his forehead or on his hand, 10 he will also drink from the wine of God's anger, that has been mixed undiluted in the cup of His wrath. And he will be tormented in fire and brimstone before the holy angels and before the Lamb. 11 And the smoke of their torment ascends forever and ever. So the ones who worship the Beast and his image have no rest, day and night, even anyone who accepts the mark of his name (Revelation 14.9-11).

The blasphemy of the Holy Spirit, the sin that cannot be forgiven, is the worship of the Beast and his image and taking his mark. John's concluding remarks of his first letter identified this sin as "sin to death:"

> If anyone should see his brother sin *a* sin not to death, he will ask and He will give him life, to the ones who do not sin to death. There is sin to death. I do not say that he should ask about that (1 John 5.16).

John wrote one sin led to death, the blasphemy of the Holy Spirit, taking the mark of the Beast. There is no point in asking the Lord to give life for committing this sin for He declared it would never be forgiven.

Paul warned the Jews about this sin in Hebrews:

> 4 It is impossible for those who were once enlightened, who tasted of the heavenly gift, and became partakers of the Holy Spirit, 5 and tasted the excellence of God's word, the powers of the coming age, 6 and fall away, to renew again to repentance, since they are recrucifying to themselves

> the Son of the God and subjecting Him to public shame (Hebrews 6.4-6).[2]

When Paul wrote about the Tribulation in 2 Thessalonians 2.7, he included the definite article with lawlessness, agreeing with what Jesus said and John wrote. But a case *cannot* be made that when Paul included the definite article with lawlessness, he always associated it with the Tribulation for Romans 4.7 and 6.19 have the article and are not Tribulation passages.

The two descriptions, "the man of the lawlessness" and "the son of the destruction" may describe different phases of the Beast's rule—the former to the first three and a half years in which the Beast is human and the latter to the last three and a half years, when he becomes superhuman, indwelt by Satan.

At the midpoint of the Tribulation the Beast is killed. The world thinks he is dead. Miraculously, Satan revives him and indwells him (Revelation 13.3-4). The description, "the son of the destruction," is a technical title. It denotes one whom Satan indwells. Two people are so identified, Judas (John 17.12 cf. John 13.27) and the Beast.

Why are these descriptors used? The phrase "the man of the lawlessness" indicates the Beast will not only demand to be worshiped as God but will overthrow what has been accepted as natural law and legal precedent throughout history (Daniel 7.25).

Excursus: Transhumanism and Transgenderism

The stage is being set for the future events of the Tribulation by current movements. Key components of what will come can be seen in the pursuits of transhumanism and transgenderism. The former seeks to change our identity from beings created in God's image to beings made in the image of man (or Satan). Transhumanists state their goal is "to change who you

---

[2] A fuller treatment is in the author's *Understanding the Jewish Writings: An Examination of Hebrews, James, 1-2 Peter, 1-3 John, Jude, and Revelation.*

are," to change our essential nature. They seek to do this with gene editing, nanotechnologies, drug technologies, altering DNA, and artificial intelligence.

Transgenderism's goal is to overthrow the foundation of all biology: maleness and femaleness. Genesis states God created humanity in His image, male and female (Genesis 1.27). God created every living organism, animal and vegetable, "after its kind," לְמִינוֹ, (Genesis 1.11-12, 21, 24-25). Thus, God created two sexes, male and female, and set biological boundaries for each kind (why dogs and cats cannot mate). Transgenderists wish to hybridize humanity and animals, to change the differences among the sexes. With the transhumanists, they wish to create humanity in their own image and modify mankind to serve them and their purposes. Those who wish to remove the biological boundaries God has established are in rebellion against Him. Like Satan, they wish to replace God and think they can become gods (Satan's original lie to Eve, Genesis 3.5).

Current transhumanism and transgenderism programs continue, but with far greater sophistication, the late 19th and early 20th century Eugenics crusade. Promoted by evolutionists and many intellectuals, eugenics' racist approach led to forced sterilization and human experimentation. Individuals such as Margaret Sanger and George Bernard Shaw were avid proponents of it. The Nazis embraced it and Joseph Mengele being it most infamous practitioner. Their ideas have revived and are being pursued in university and government labs with advanced technologies.

Such activity is not new. It occurred in Noah's generation. Fallen angels had sexual relations with women to whom were born giants (Genesis 6.1-4). Biological manipulation also occurred among animals in creating chimera. These actions were the source of the mythologies of gods, demi-gods, and hybrid animals. Because these activities threatened the human race and animal creation with total corruption, God brought the Flood. It destroyed all human life except eight persons, Noah and his immediate family, free from biological corruption, and all land-based animal life, except animals on the ark. Such devastating divine judgment reveals the scale of the danger transhuman and transgenic activities were to humanity and all life.

Genesis 6.4 reveals more transgenic activities occurred after the Flood. When the Jews came to the promised land, they encountered giants. They were terrified by them and refused to trust God and enter the land as He instructed. The majority report of the spies declared they were like grasshoppers to the giants (Numbers 13.32-33). As a result, Moses' generation wandered in the desert forty years and died.

God instructed Moses that the Jews were to completely destroy certain peoples when they entered the promised land (Deuteronomy 7.1-2, 20.17). They were to kill their livestock also. Many have tried to explain this harsh command, but the explanations fall short. More was going on than that they were God's enemies, that this was a holy war against exceedingly immoral people engaged in worshipping false gods and committing child sacrifice. This was true, but such explanations do not address the larger problem. Nor do they explain God's command to kill the animals.

The only adequate explanation is that both human and animal bloodlines were again becoming corrupted by fallen angels who produced giants with women. While the Biblical text does not address animal modification, extra-biblical texts such as the *Book of Jasher* and *Book of Jubilees*,[3] reveal genetic modification was occurring among animals, resulting in chimera. Such hybrid animals are seen in every culture's mythology. Is this possible? Solomon wrote:

> 9 The thing that has been, it is that which will be; and that which is done is that which will be done: and there is no new thing under the sun. 10 Is there anything whereof it may be said, See, this is new? it has been

---

[3] *Book of Jasher* 4.18, 36.30-35, 61.14-17; *Book of Jubilees* 5.1-5, 7.21-25.

> already of old time, which was before us (Ecclesiastes 1.9-10).

God ordered Saul to kill the inhabitants of the land and their livestock. He failed to obey (1 Samuel 13.13-14; 15.1-31). As a result, God removed his kingship and made David king. David showed his character by killing the giant Goliath, and after becoming king, killing all the giants. His obedience in this area was the primary reason God described him as a man after His heart (Acts 13.22, cf. 1 Samuel 13.14).

The most plausible explanation for God's command to kill the livestock was that they were being genetically modified. What had occurred in Noah's day was occurring again—angelic interference with the human and the animal creation. Fallen angels had knowledge of how to modify human and animal genomes. As God protected and saved the human race and the animal creation by the Flood, Israel became His agent to protect humanity and the animal creation by killing the Canaanites, giants, and designated animals. This was part of their role to bless that Gentiles God gave in the Abrahamic Covenant.

God spoke about this matter in Eden after Adam and the woman ate from the forbidden tree. The text reads:

> 14 And the LORD God said to the serpent, Because you have done this, you are cursed above all cattle, and above every beast of the field; upon your belly will you go, and dust will you eat all the days of your life:
> 15 And I will put enmity between you and the woman, and between your seed and her seed; it will bruise your head, and you will bruise his heel (Genesis 3.14-15).

The Lord addressed Satan, not a snake. Eve conversed with Satan, who is described as the Snake or Dragon throughout Scripture. Created as God's most glorious creature, God told Satan his destiny for lying and tempting the woman to sin would be humiliation and shame, metaphorically expressed as cursed above all cattle, crawling on his belly, eating dust.

The Lord also told Satan He would put enmity between Satan and the woman, between her seed and Satan's seed. The word "seed," זֶרַע, means "offspring," "descendants," "children." The specific prophetic reference was to Christ and by extension, those who believe in Him. Mankind defeats Satan through Christ, the God-man but Eve probably thought Cain was the fulfillment of the Lord's words based on Genesis 4.1.

What is meant by "Satan's seed?" It has both metaphorical and physical senses. Metaphorically, it describes those allied with Satan who have rebelled against God and those who reject God and His salvation. Jesus told His Jewish opponents that their father was the Devil (John 8.44). The physical offspring of Satan includes the giants, the hybrid angel-human beings born through the sexual union of angels and women. Satan's intent was to corrupt the human bloodline so no one could qualify as "human" as a redeemer. In the future, it will include those who take the mark of the Beast. Satan also biologically corrupted the animal creation (perhaps because animals were used for animal sacrifices). Satan hates everything God has created and wishes to twist and corrupt it to his design and purposes.

This sheds light on what Paul wrote the Corinthians:

> Because of this, the woman ought to have *a sign of* authority on the head because of the angels (1 Corinthians 11.10).

Woman's "sign of authority," head covering, in the divine order is that she is part of mankind, from Adam, under his authority and shelter. The significance of the sign to angels is one of protection, a warning that women are "off limits" sexually and a reminder that God created everything after its kind. Severe judgment and consequences fall on those who violate this divine order. While Sodom and Gomorrah and the surrounding cities practiced great immorality, the primary reason for their destruction was for violating sexual boundaries. This was the context of Peter statement in 2 Peter 2.4-6.

The Lord declared that when He returns, the world will again be like Noah's time (Matthew 24.37-39). The mark of the Beast will change a person's biological makeup from being made in God's image to being made in the Beast's image. Paul's words in Hebrews 6.4-6 are more clearly understood in this light. He warned that one who "falls away" cannot be renewed again to repentance. Why?

Paul's statement is contrary to everything found elsewhere in Scripture. The Scriptures reveal that no matter how heinous a sin, one can repent, turn to God, and gain salvation. But Paul's words indicate an exception exists for one who "falls away." What does this mean and how is this possible?

The most plausible explanation is that if a person takes the Beast's mark alters his DNA, changes his genetic code so that he can no longer repent. We are composed of body, soul, and spirit. Our physical makeup is united with our immaterial being. If the building blocks (genes, DNA, etc.) are significantly altered, such a change can remove the ability to repent and respond to God. In essence, one is changed so one is no longer in the image of God. This seems to be what the mark of the Beast will do. It will alter one to be a creation made in the image of the Beast. The adjective, ἀδύνατος, translated "impossible," in Hebrews 6.4 denotes "inability," "powerlessness." Therefore, one *cannot* be renewed again to repentance for one no longer possesses the equipment to do so. The Beast's mark alters one so that one becomes a creation of Satan—Satan's seed. This may seem incredible but Paul's words are clear—one who falls away cannot be renewed again to repentance.

Revelation 14.9-11 warns that anyone who accepts the Beast's mark will suffer eternal punishment. Taking the Beast's mark was what Paul meant with his warning about "falling away." The Beast's mark dooms all who accept it to eternal punishment. It explains Jesus' stern warning about the blasphemy of the Holy Spirit (worship of the Beast, his image, and taking his mark) and about enduring to the end to be saved" (Matthew 24.13).[4]

One who refuses to worship the Beast and take his mark cannot buy or sell and will be killed (Revelation 13.15-17). Taking the Beast's mark in the Tribulation will be a choice. Jesus taught about this with His statement about denying or acknowledging Him (Matthew 10.32-33) and when He instructed that one who finds his life will lose it and loses his life for His sake will find it (Matthew 10.39).

Satan is the source behind eugenics, transhumanism, and transgenderism. He wishes to corrupt God's image, to change who we are, to make us into beings made in his image, to enslave us to worship and serve him. Most involved in these movements do not understand this or believe in Satan or God. They have their own agendas. But the leaders who plan, finance, and promote these movements know better. They knowingly worship and serve Satan.

God created mankind in His image and all creatures after its kind. Those engaged in altering God's design are in rebellion against Him. The eugenic, transhuman, and transgender movements of today are a preview of the horrors of the Tribulation. The "lawlessness" of which Jesus and Paul warned becomes fully manifest in mankind's worship of Satan and taking the Beast's mark, sealing one's eternal doom.

The phrase, "the son of the destruction" (verse 3), describes the Beast indwelt by Satan. Satan brings death to all he touches. Revelation 9.11 states:

> They have *a* king over them, the angel of the Abyss. His name in Hebrew *is* Abaddon, and in the Greek, he has the name Apollyon.

---

[4] This subject is explored in the author's *Understanding the Jewish Writings: An Examination of Hebrews, James, 1-2 Peter, 1-3 John, Jude, and Revelation.*

Satan is the king of the creatures imprisoned in the Abyss. Revelation 9.1-12 describes his release of these creatures and he is identified in verse 11 as the angel of the Abyss, named "Abaddon," אֲבַדּוֹן, and "Apollyon," Ἀπολλύων. Both mean "Destroyer." Revelation 9 and 12 describe the same time period, the mid-point of the Tribulation. After God's righteous angels defeat and remove Satan and his forces from heaven (Revelation 12), Satan descends into the Abyss (Revelation 9) and releases these transgenic creatures. After this, the Beast is killed and Satan will revive and indwell him. The Beast becomes his "son," "the son of the destruction," Satan's "seed." The Beast becomes the Satan-man, even as Jesus is the God-man. Satan is the great imitator and counterfeiter of God.

Verse 4 describes the Beast as "the one who opposes and exalts himself above every named god or object of worship." The Beast will stop the daily animal sacrifices the Jews have been offering for the previous three and a half years in the rebuilt Temple (Daniel 8.11-13, 11.31, 12.11). After this, he will seat himself in the Temple and "display himself: that he is God." In the participial phrase "display himself," ἀποδεικνύντα ἑαυτὸν, the verb ἀποδείκνυμι is used only by Luke and Paul (Acts 2.22, 25.7; 1 Corinthians 4.9; 2 Thessalonians 2.4). It means to declare, exhibit, or prove something. The Beast, indwelt by Satan, will use his revival, overcoming death, to claim he is God. This counterfeit resurrection and the signs and miracles of the False Prophet (Revelation 13.11-15) will convince the world of his claim.

Jesus described the Beast declaring himself God and desecrating the Temple as "the abomination of the desolation," τὸ βδέλυγμα τῆς ἐρημώσεως, and instructed Jews to flee to the mountains when they saw it (Matthew 24.15; Mark 13.14). The Lord had in mind what Daniel wrote:

> 36 And the king will do according to his will; and he will exalt himself, and magnify himself above every god, and will speak marvelous things against the God of gods,

> and will prosper until the indignation be accomplished: for that that is determined will be done. [37] Neither will he regard the God of his fathers, nor the desire of women, nor regard any god: for he will magnify himself above all (Daniel 11.36-37; cf. Daniel 8.13, 9.26-27, 11.31, 12.11).

---

[5] Do you not recall, when I was still with you, I kept telling you these things?
[6] And you know what now restrains *him*, so he might be revealed in his time.
[7] For the secret of the lawlessness is already at work, only the One who now restrains *him* will continue until it should be done out of *the* way.
[8] And then the lawless one will be revealed, whom the Lord[5] will slay[6] by the breath of His mouth and abolish by the appearance of His coming,
[9] whose coming is after *the* working of Satan, by every power, and by signs, and false wonders,
[10] and by every deceit of the unrighteousness to those who perish, because they did not accept the love of the truth so they might be saved.
[11] And because of this, the God will send them *a* supernatural work of deceit, so that they believe in the lie,
[12] so all these might be judged, who did not believe in the truth, but delighted in the unrighteousness.

Comment:

Verses 5-12: Paul wrote in verse 5, "Do you not recall, when I was still with you, I kept telling you these things?" After the Thessalonians believed the gospel, Paul taught them the Pre-Tribulation Rapture and about the advent of the Beast. One of the great principles of teaching is "repetition is the mother of learning." Truths must be repeated to become rooted into one's thinking. Satan, the god of this age, controls most of the world's narrative, a narrative of deceit, a

---

[5] Some manuscripts have "Jesus," Ἰησοῦς.
[6] Some manuscripts have the verb ἀνελεῖ, "slay" while others have ἀναλώσει, "consume."

magic show. God's word is the counter-narrative to Satan's false reality. Paul repeated and elaborated on what he taught previously and what he wrote in his first letter to firmly establish the Thessalonians.

Verses 6-8 further explain verses 1-4. Paul declared in verse 6, "And now, you know what restrains *him*, so he might be revealed in his time." The participle κατέχον, "restrains" (present active neuter) is transitive, needing an object—"him." With the neuter definite article τό, the text reads, "the thing that restrains him," or "what restrains him." What "thing" retrains the appearance of the Beast, "so he might be revealed in his time?" The Church restrains the Beast. When God removes the Church with the Rapture, the Beast can then appear. Daniel's 70th week cannot begin until God removes the Church.

Verse 7 states, "for the secret of the lawlessness is already at work," τὸ γὰρ μυστήριον ἤδη ἐνεργεῖται τῆς ἀνομίας. Again, the noun "lawlessness" has the definite article. It is "the lawlessness" associated with the Beast and the Tribulation. What did Paul mean by "the secret of the lawlessness is already at work?"

Satan is brilliant but much of God's plan remains hidden to him. He does not know when God will complete the Church. God's creation of the Church, the body of Christ, was a complete surprise to Satan—a secret according to Ephesians 3. Because Satan does not know when God will complete His Church, he must constantly identify and prepare individuals to serve as the Beast. Paul wrote this was occurring in his day: "the secret of the lawlessness is already at work." It has continued throughout history. Satan likely identifies several persons in every generation.

Paul continued, "only the One who now restrains *him* will continue until it should be removed out of *the* way." The participle "restrains" is repeated from verse 6 and is transitive, requiring an object—"him." What is different, however, is that in verse 6 it is neuter, i.e., "what restrains," τὸ κατέχον. Here, the participle is masculine, ὁ κατέχων, "the one restraining,"

In verse 6, Paul wrote a *thing* prevents the advent of the Beast. In verse 7, he wrote a *person* prevents the advent of the Beast. The *thing* preventing the advent of the Beast is the presence of the Church, the body of Christ. The *person* preventing the advent of the Beast is the Lord. He controls the Church's presence and completion. He is "the Restrainer."

Continuing verse 7, what did Paul mean by the expression ἕως ἐκ μέσου γένηται? All translations render this "until he is removed out of the way." The verb γένηται is the present middle or passive subjunctive, third person singular of the verb γίνομαι, which means "become, happen, do, fulfill." The subjunctive mood expresses potential or contingency. A third person singular can be "he, she, or it." Despite other translations, the better rendering is "until it should be done out of the way." The "it" is the Church.

Verses 6 and 7 thus further expand verse 3, where Paul wrote the "the departure (ἡ ἀποστασία) must come first and then the man of the lawlessness should be revealed." Verse 6 denotes "what" restrains the advent of the Beast, the Church and verse 7 denotes "who" restrains him. Only after the Lord removes His Church can the Beast appear and the Tribulation begin. These verses forcefully, and clearly, proclaim the Pre-Tribulation Rapture. How can anyone deny it?

Thus, Paul wrote that after the Lord removes His Church, "And then the lawless one will be revealed" (verse 8). Once Satan sees the Church removed, he knows God has made a strategic move and the way is open to bring in the Beast. It is unclear if this occurs immediately after the Rapture or whether a number of years will pass. It will probably depend on the stage of preparation of the Beast and the political climate. Throughout the Bible, forty years has been a time of testing. Satan is the great imitator of God and he may identify and prepare his man for thirty-three years imitating the Lord. Once the Beast signs the treaty of Daniel 9.27, seven years would remain to finish forty years.

Paul described the fate of the Beast, "whom the Lord will slay by the breath of His mouth and abolish by the appearance of His coming" (verse 8). The Lord's appearing will terrify and devastate those warring against Him. David described this in Psalm 2:

> [1] Why do the heathen rage, and the people imagine a vain thing? [2] The kings of the earth set themselves, and the rulers take counsel together, against the LORD, and against his anointed, saying, [3] Let us break their bands asunder, and cast away their cords from us. [4] He that sits in the heavens will laugh: the LORD will have them in derision. [5] Then will he speak to them in his wrath, and vex them in his sore displeasure (Psalm 2.2-8).

At Armageddon, the Lord crushes His enemies: Satan, the Beast, the False Prophet, and the forces allied with them. Most of humanity has chosen to worship Satan and identify with the Beast by taking his mark. As they see the Lord returning, they know they are doomed. They "rage" and "imagine a vain thing."[7] John described how every socio-economic group reacts at Christ's return.

> [15] And the kings of the earth, and the moguls, and the rich, and the commanders, and the powerful, and every servant, and every freeman, hid themselves in the caves and in the rocks of the mountains. [16] And they said to the mountains and the rocks, Fall on us and hide us from the face of the One who sits on the throne and from the wrath of the Lamb [17] for the great day of His wrath has come and who can stand (Revelation 6.15-17; cf. Zephaniah 1.14)?

Rage, irrationality, and terror such as mankind has never experienced characterizes the world as they see Christ return. Paul wrote the Jews:

---

[7] Psalm 2 describes Christ's 1st and 2nd Advent, Tribulation, and Millennial kingdom, summarizing God's prophetic plan.

> It is a terrifying thing to fall into the hands of the living God (Hebrews 10.31).

John described the Lord's return, thus:

> Behold, He comes with the clouds. And every eye will see Him, even those who pierced Him. And all the peoples of the earth will wail because of Him. Yes! Amen (Revelation 1.7)!

Having withheld His wrath for millennia, divine judgment finally falls. Jeremiah wrote:

> Therefore prophesy against them all these words, and say to them, The LORD will roar from on high, and utter his voice from his holy habitation; he will mightily roar on his habitation; he will give a shout, as they that tread the grapes, against all the inhabitants of the earth (Jeremiah 25.30).

At His first advent, especially at the cross, He was submissive, meek and lowly. He allowed Himself to be tortured and abused. No more. He returns in glory and power to crush all who worship Satan.

Structurally, verse 3a parallels verse 7 and verse 3b parallels verse 8:

Verse 3a: Do not let anyone deceive you in any way. For the departure must come first

Verse 7: For the secret of the lawlessness is already at work, only the One who now restrains *him* will continue until it should be done out of *the* way.

Verse 3b: and then the man of the lawlessness should be revealed, the son of the destruction,

Verse 8: And then the lawless one will be revealed, whom the Lord will slay by the breath of His mouth and abolish by the appearance of His coming,

---

The last part of verse 8 states, "will slay by the breath of His mouth and abolish by the appearance of His coming." The two phrases exhibit Hebrew parallelism. When the Lord returns, He utterly defeats the Beast. Some manuscripts have the verb ἀνελεῖ, "slay" and others ἀναλώσει, "consume." The former verb is used much more frequently, almost always by Luke and once by Paul (Hebrews 10.9). The latter verb is found only in Luke 9.54 and Galatians 5.15. Whatever the autograph read, the message is the clear: the Lord completely defeats Satan, the Beast, and the False Prophet. The expression "by the breath of His mouth, τῷ πνεύματι τοῦ στόματος αὐτοῦ, is an idiom for the Lord's speaking—He is the Word of God. All He need do to defeat His enemies is speak.

In the last phrase, "abolish by the appearance of His coming," the verb translated "abolish," καταργέω, means to annul or render someone or something powerless or ineffective. It is used twenty-seven times, always by Paul, except for once by Luke. The Lord ends the Beast's power. The noun translated "appearance," ἐπιφάνεια, is only used by Paul (2 Thessalonians 2.8; 1 Timothy 6.14; 2 Timothy 1.10, 4.1, 8; Titus 2.13), always for Christ's glorious appearing. The Lord's appearing in glory with His saints and all the holy angels will be marvelous beyond compare. The Lord has hundreds of millions of angels (Daniel 7.10; Revelation 5.11) and heaven and earth have never witnessed such an event. Those who love Him will rejoice; those who hate Him are terrified.

Verses 9-10 describe how the Beast will come and how and why he is accepted. He comes "after the working of Satan." Paul alone used the noun translated "working," ἐνέργεια, always for supernatural power (Ephesians 1.19, 3.7, 4.16; Philippians 3.21; Colossians 1.29, 2.12; 2 Thessalonians 2.9, 11). Satan prepares the man who steps into the role of the Beast and installs him by supernatural influence and power.

The great event Satan will use to convince the world the Beast is God will be by reviving him from death.

This revival is followed by signs from the False Prophet. John described these:

> [13] And he performs great signs, so that he even makes fire come down from the heaven to the earth before mankind. [14] And he deceives those who live on the earth through the signs that he was allowed to perform before the Beast, by telling those live on the earth to make an image to the Beast who had the sword wound and lived. [15] And he was allowed to give breath to the Beast's image so the Beast's image could speak, and could cause as many as would not worship the Beast's image to be executed (Revelation 13.13-15).

The world under Satan in the Tribulation is total tyranny. People become convinced by powerful miracles but controlled by terror. Resisting the Beast means death. But far better to die by the Beast than to follow Satan and experience eternal death. On four occasions the Lord warned His listeners:

> For whoever should wish to save his life will lose it. But whoever should lose his life for Me will find it (Matthew 16.25; cf. Mark 8.35; Luke 9.24, 17.33).

Many save their lives in the Tribulation by taking the Beast's mark. But doing so means they lose eternal life. Losing one's life for the Lord, believing He is the Christ and refusing the Beast's mark, gains eternal life.

Despite the terror of Satan and the Beast, the Lord reminded His disciples:

> So do not be afraid of those who kill the body. They cannot kill the soul. Rather, be afraid of the One who can destroy both soul and body in hell (Matthew 10.28).

Paul continued in verse 10, "and by every deceit of the unrighteousness to those who perish, because they did not accept the love of the truth so they might be saved." Some manuscripts do not have the articular construct, τῆς ἀδικίας "of the unrighteousness" but it is probably present (as in verse 12) as it identifies a specific unrighteousness. Whether the autograph had the definite article or not, the noun is definite.

What is this unrighteousness? It is worshipping Satan and taking the Beast's mark. Why will one do this? Paul wrote that it is because one "does not accept the love of the truth." The articular "the truth," τῆς ἀληθείας, is the gospel of the kingdom.

After God removes His Church, Paul's gospel, which focuses on Christ's *work*, He died for our sins, was buried, and rose from the dead (1 Corinthians 15.1-4), will no longer be the message of salvation. The gospel of the kingdom, focuses of Christ's *identity*, who He is, the Messiah, the Son of God, and will again become the message of salvation. When Jesus addressed His disciples about the Tribulation, He declared,

> And this gospel of the kingdom will be proclaimed in all the earth for *a* testimony to all the nations. And then the end will come (Matthew 24.14).

The reason the gospel of the kingdom replaces Paul's gospel in the Tribulation and becomes the message of salvation is because the great test for humanity after God removes the Church is who is God. Satan, in the person of the Beast, will claim to be God and order everyone to worship him. Those who resist are killed (Revelation 13.15). Thus, the great test for humanity in the Tribulation is, "Is the Beast God or is Jesus of Nazareth God?" What one believes about this question determines one's eternal destiny. Paul wrote that those who refuse to believe Jesus is the Christ are those who do not accept the love of the truth "so they might be saved," εἰς τὸ σωθῆναι αὐτούς.

In verse 11, Paul explained that those who refuse to accept the love of the truth to be saved, "God will send them *a* supernatural work of deceit, so that they believe in the lie." The noun "work" in "supernatural work of deceit," ἐνέργειαν πλάνης, is the same word in verse 9, "the working of Satan." As nature abhors a vacuum, so supernature. If truth is rejected, falsehood fills the void. God respects and does not interfere with mankind's free will. Writing on this subject, Paul explained in Romans 1.18-21 that everyone knows God exists and that God reveals Himself through His creation. Most of humanity suppresses this evidence, resulting in a darkened heart. Three times, in Romans 1.24, 26, 28, Paul used the verb παραδίδωμι to declare that God allows men to have their way. He "gives over" men to deceit and error.

Paul concluded Romans 1 stating:

> Although they know the righteous decree of the God—that those who practice such things are worthy of death—they not only do them, but also agree with those practicing *them* (Romans 1.32).

We get what we want. If one wishes to know God, God will provide information for salvation. God forces salvation on no one. He cannot force anyone to love Him. He draws us, He woos us. To those who reject the gospel of the kingdom He will send a supernatural work of deceit—the Beast's signs and miracles.

What is "the lie" in verse 11? The text reads that God sends them a supernatural work of deceit "so that they believe in the lie," τῷ ψεύδει. Almost all translations omit the definite article, a critical error. The definite article with the noun denotes a particular lie. It is that the Beast is God. It may also include Satan's original lie—humanity can become as gods if they follow him.

Those who believe in the lie, do this, "so all these might be judged, who did not believe in the truth, but delighted in the unrighteousness" (verse 12). Note the contrast between "in the lie," τῷ ψεύδει, (verse 11), "in the unrighteousness," τῇ ἀδικίᾳ, (verse 12) and "in the truth," τῇ ἀληθείᾳ, (verse 12). All the nouns are articular. "The lie" and "the unrighteousness" denote worship of the Beast. "The truth" is the gospel of the kingdom, Jesus is the Messiah, the Son of God.

Why does God allow the Tribulation? What is its purpose? Some things are learned at an intellectual level. But most learning comes from experience. God told Adam and the woman if they ate from the tree of the knowledge of good and evil, they would die. God gave them intellection knowledge. They ate anyway. While tragic, this gave them a deeper understanding, experiential knowledge, about what God told them.

The Tribulation demonstrates, as never before, who we are apart from God. Mankind has committed almost unimaginable horrors throughout history. The Tribulation reveals mankind's heart of darkness as never before, worshipping Satan and destroying God's creation. The population will probably be reduced a thousand-fold. Men and women will lose their identity as being made in God's image to become beings made in Satan's image. The great lesson God shows the angelic host and mankind in the Tribulation is that everything apart from God is death. Those whom God condemns condemn themselves by rejecting the truth.

Stand Fast in Paul's Doctrines

13 Now we ought to thank the God always for you, brethren, beloved by *the* Lord, that the God chose you from the beginning for salvation, by *the* sanctification of *the* Spirit and by faith in *the* truth.
14 For which He also called you through our gospel to possess *the* glory of our Lord Jesus Christ.
15 So then, brethren, stand fast, and hold the teachings that you were taught, whether through word or through letter from us.
16 Now our Lord Jesus Christ Himself and our God and Father, the One who loved us and gave us eternal encouragement and good hope in grace,
17 may He encourage and strengthen your hearts in every good word and work.[8]

Comment:

Verses 13-17: Thanksgiving characterized Paul's ministry and the obligatory "we ought to thank" ὀφείλομεν εὐχαριστεῖν, expresses how we should thank God for believers who are "beloved by the

---

[8] Some manuscripts read "every work and good word."

Lord." The reason for thanksgiving is because God chose them "from *the* beginning," ἀπ' αρχῆς, for salvation and this was by the sanctification of the Spirit and by faith in the truth. God's chose believers based on foreknowledge (cf. Romans 8.29-30).

God inhabits eternity, outside time. For Him, past, present, and future are *now*. God predestines (the verb προορίζω is used only of believers when used of persons) believers to a *destiny*: to be conformed into Christ's image (Romans 8.29). God's foreknowledge governs His predestining, calling, justifying, and glorifying believers (Romans 8.30). God gives every person many opportunities to know Him and knows how a person will respond.

God always takes the initiative in salvation. After Adam and Eve sinned, eating the forbidden fruit, they hid. God went looking for them. This divine initiative is unique with every person. God presents truth, His presence, knowledge of Himself, in many different ways to each person. God deals with us uniquely. If a person responds to His wooing, He provides everything needed for salvation. Each person has an equal opportunity for God is not limited or constrained by geography, distance, language, or other barriers. Jesus declared that with God, nothing is impossible (Matthew 19.26; Luke 1.37).

Salvation involves both divine and human wills: God's drawing and man's response, noted in verse 13, "by *the* sanctification of *the* Spirit and by faith in *the* truth." "Sanctification of the Sprit" is the divine action. "Faith in the truth" is the human response. Thus, "chose you from the beginning for salvation" is governed by God's foreknowledge of what occurs when divine and human wills interact.

Paul continued in verse 14, describing how God had chosen them: "He also called you through our gospel to possess *the* glory of our Lord Jesus Christ," εἰς περιποίησιν δόξης τοῦ κυρίου ἡμῶν Ἰησοῦ Χριστοῦ. The Thessalonians came to know Christ through Paul's gospel. Paul's expression means when one believes Paul's gospel one comes to possess Christ's glory. His glory is our inheritance as God's heir and Christ's joint-heir (Romans 8.17). God is surrounded by glory but Christ's greatest inheritance and glory are those who trust and love Him. We share that glory.

As a result of believing his gospel, Paul urged believers to "stand fast, and hold the teachings that you were taught, whether through word or through letter from us" (verse 15).

The verb στήκω, "stand fast," is found eight times in the New Testament, all but one used by Paul (cf. Mark 11.25; Romans 14.4; 1 Corinthians 16.13; Galatians 5.1; Philippians 1.27, 4.1; 1 Thessalonians 3.8; 2 Thessalonians 2.15). Most of the time, Paul used it as a present active imperative, as here (cf. 1 Corinthians 16.13; Galatians 5.1; Philippians 4.1; 2 Thessalonians 2.15). He wrote the Corinthians to "stand fast in the faith," the Galatians, to "stand fast in the freedom in which Christ set us free," the Philippians, to "stand fast in the Lord." In this verse, Paul commanded the Thessalonians to "stand fast and hold the teachings," στήκετε καὶ κρατεῖτε τὰς παραδόσεις, they were taught. While the noun παράδοσις, is often translated "tradition," the rest of the verse, "word or through letter from us," indicates Paul meant what he taught or wrote (cf. 2 Thessalonians 3.6).

Paul's letters contain *all* Church doctrine. We learn nothing of Church doctrine or our position in Christ as members of His body from the Gospels or from the writings of James, Peter, John, or Jude. While all Scripture is God-breathed and beneficial for instruction (2 Timothy 3.16; Romans 15.4; 1 Corinthians 10.11), Paul's letters alone are addressed to members of the Church, the body of Christ. Paul commanded the Thessalonians to stand fast in the things said or written "from us" (verse 15), a nosism for himself. Again, he did not say the things taught or written in the Gospels or the writings of Peter, James, Jude, or John. For members of the Church, the body of Christ, Paul's letters are the sole source of God's salvation and the key to living a victorious Christian life. Most churches spend most of their time in the Gospels. They may increase in numbers, but without the teaching from Paul's letters, they are weak and unable to grow spiritually.

Verses 16-17 identify who God is to us as members of the Church and what He has done for us. He is "our Lord Jesus Christ Himself and our God and Father." He is "the One who loved us and gave us eternal encouragement and good hope in grace." Despite troubles, we have an indescribable destiny as joint-heirs with Christ and eternal life. Such knowledge is our encouragement and hope.

In verse 17, Paul asked that the God who has done this, "may He encourage and strengthen your hearts in every good word and work." The verbs, "encourage" and "strengthen" are in the optative mood, found only sixty-eight times in the New Testament, which Paul used thirty-one times. This mood expresses a strong wish or desire. In the Thessalonian letters, he used it nine times (1 Thessalonians 3.11, 12, 5.23; 2 Thessalonians 2.17, 3.5, 3.16). Paul used it fourteen times in his expression μὴ γένοιτο, translated by the KJV as "God forbid," which I have translated as "Never!" Paul used this as his strongest negation. Who Christ is and what He has done for us should govern our words and deeds.

Paul expanded the thought of verses 16-17 in his paean to the Romans in chapter 8:

> [31]Therefore, what will we say about these things? If the God *is* for us, who *is* against us? [32] Indeed, He who did not spare His own Son, but delivered Him for us all, how will He not also with Him give us all things (Romans 8.31-32)?

2 Thessalonians 3

Paul's Request for Prayer

1 As to the rest, brethren, pray for us, that the word of the Lord may spread quickly and may be glorified, just as also with you,
2 and that we might be delivered from the perverse and evil men. For not all have the faith.
3 But the Lord is faithful, who will establish and protect you from the Evil One.
4 Now we are confident in *the* Lord about you, that you do and will do the things we command.
5 Now may the Lord direct your hearts to the love of the God and to the endurance of the Christ.

Comment:

Verses 1-5: Given what Paul wrote before, he now began his closing remarks—"as to the rest," τὸ λοιπὸν, asking them to pray for himself and those with him. His specific request was for God's word to spread quickly and be glorified. Paul used the verb translated "quickly," τρέχω, most often for running (cf. Romans 9.16; 1 Corinthians 9.24, 26; Galatians 2.2, 5.7; Philippians 2.16). The verb translated "glorified," δοξάζω, conveyed the desire that others might receive God's word with honor and praise, even as they.

Paul continued his prayer request in verse 2, that they "might be delivered from the perverse and evil men." The articular nouns denote men of this particular category or class—perverse and evil. The verb translated "delivered," ῥύομαι, is the same as in 1 Thessalonians 1.10, where he wrote the Lord will "rescue" the Church from the Tribulation. As in that passage, Paul used the preposition ἀπό, "away from."

He then declared, the reason: "for not all have the faith." Most translations render this as, "for not all have faith" but such a rendering is ambiguous and does not clearly communicate Paul's meaning. The text has the definite article with the noun, "the faith," ἡ πίστις. Without translating the article, the reader cannot tell whether Paul meant the act of believing or what is believed. The noun with the definite article leaves no doubt. He meant what was believed, his gospel, his doctrines.

Having requested their prayers, Paul contrasted men who do not have the faith with the Lord who is faithful (πιστὸς δέ ἐστιν ὁ κύριος) and would strengthen and protect them "from the Evil One" (verse 3). The phrase, ἀπὸ τοῦ πονηροῦ, employs the preposition ἀπό, "away from" and the articular masculine noun denotes an individual—"the Evil One," Satan. The verbs, στηρίξει and φυλάξει are futures and mean "will strengthen" or "will establish" and "will watch over," "will protect." Given the content of this letter and 1 Thessalonians, Paul's primary meaning of "from the Evil One" was their physical removal from his presence by means of the Rapture. Paul used the preposition ἀπό as he had in Romans 5.9 and 1 Thessalonians 1.10, both Rapture passages. In a general sense, Paul could also have meant God would protect them from the false teaching that they were in the Tribulation.

In verse 4, Paul expressed confidence they would continue what they were doing and do the things he commanded. Paul then blessed them in verse 5, that the Lord would direct their hearts "to the love of the God and to the endurance of the Christ." The genitive, "love of the God" is most likely a subjective genitive, God's love for them but could also be plenary, having both subjective and objective senses, i.e., God's love for them and their love for God. God initiates love and as we respond to His love, we love him (cf. 1 John 4.19). The same can be said for the genitive, "the endurance of the Christ." It most likely is a subjective genitive, meaning Christ's endurance, enduring the cross, paying for our sins but could also have a plenary sense, that one who contemplates Christ's endurance is motivated to endure for Him (cf. Hebrews 12.3).

Command to Disassociate from Believers Not Following Paul

6 Now we command you brethren, in *the* name of our Lord Jesus Christ, to withdraw from every brother who walks disorderly and not according to the teaching which you received from us.
7 For yourselves know how you must imitate us for we did not act disorderly among you
8 or eat bread from anyone without payment, but by labor and toil, we worked night and day not to burden any of you.
9 Not because we do have *the* authority, but that we might give ourselves as *an* example for you to imitate us.

Comment:

Verses 6-9: Paul commanded members of the Church, the body of Christ, in Christ's name, to disassociate from and avoid believers who walked disorderly and did not follow his teaching. Paul's command was "in the name of our Lord Jesus Christ," a statement denoting that this command came directly from the ascended Lord, not one Paul initiated on his own. The command to disassociate "from every brother," ἀπὸ παντὸς ἀδελφοῦ, means to physically distance oneself from disorderly believers or believers who do not follow Paul's teaching. It is a strong command, and is repeated in verse 14.

1 and 2 Thessalonians were Paul's first letters. That Paul would give such a strong command early in his ministry shows the strict orders the Lord had given Paul about his commission. As such, Paul repeated these commands in later letters. He wrote the Romans:

> 17 Now I urge you, brethren, to identify those who cause the divisions and the offences contrary to the doctrine that you learned and avoid them. 18 For such do not serve our Lord Jesus Christ but their own appetites. And through the smooth-talk and flattery they deceive the hearts of the naïve (Romans 16.17-18).

To Timothy, he wrote:

> 3 If anyone teaches another doctrine and does not agree to sound words, to those of our Lord Jesus Christ, and with the teaching about godliness, 4 he is proud and understands nothing, but *has a* sickly interest in disputes and verbal quarrels from which come envy, strife, slander, evil suspicions, 5 bickerings of men who have corrupted their mind and are destitute of the truth, who think the godliness is *a* means of gain. Withdraw from such[1] (1 Timothy 6.3-5).

Note that Paul wrote that what he taught were the words "of our Lord Jesus Christ."

To Titus, he wrote:

> 10 Avoid *a* heretic after *a* first and second admonition, 11 because you know that such *a* man has corrupted himself and sins, since he is self-condemned (Titus 3.10-11).

Paul instructed Titus with how to deal with a heretic, αἱρετικός, one who was factious, who taught contrary to his teachings. He told Titus to admonish such a person. If, after a second admonition, the person failed to correct his teaching, believers were to avoid him.

Such strong commands must be understood by recognizing that Paul is to the Church what Abraham and Moses were to the Jews. Abraham was the origin of the Jews and Moses their lawgiver. Paul was God's handpicked agent whom God commissioned to begin the Church and reveal all its doctrines, which Paul called secrets. Christendom's greatest theological failure has been in not recognizing this fact.

Instead of teaching from Paul's letters, the vast majority in Christendom spend most of their time in the Gospels, in Jesus' earthly ministry. They do not

---

[1] Some manuscripts do not have this command, ἀφίστασο ἀπὸ τῶν τοιούτων.

comprehend Jesus ministered to Israel, under the Mosaic Law, to fulfill God's covenant, prophetic program (cf. Romans 15.8). They do not realize that the Gospels are Old Testament and that nothing in them concerns the Church. The Church is not under the Mosaic Law but under Grace (Romans 6.14). The Church has no prophecy associated with it. The Church did not exist in Jesus' earthly ministry. How could He communicate Church teaching when the Church did not exist?

This failure is the primary reason churches are weak, confused, and divided. It does not matter if they are Roman Catholic, Eastern Orthodox, Protestant, Baptist, Methodist, Anglican, Presbyterian, Methodist, etc. All have failed. All are confused. The existence of these denominations and thousands more prove Christendom's confusion. If believers and churches in Christendom believed and obeyed the ascended Lord's instructions to Paul, such fragmentation would not exist. Christendom would be united in Christ, not divided. At the end of his ministry Paul wrote all Asia deserted him (2 Timothy 1.15). This began the great apostasy that exists today.

Seminaries, churches, pastors, teachers obedient to Christ spend most of their time learning from and teaching Paul letters, instructing fellow believers in the great Church truths revealed in them. Believers obedient to Christ in our present age avoid churches that fail to do this. Paul wrote such church bodies "do not serve our Lord Jesus Christ but their own appetites," are "proud and understand nothing," and are "heretics." This is a hard saying. But we must remember each of us will stand before the Lord one day regarding our faithfulness to Him.

In verse 7, Paul reminded the Thessalonians that they knew how they must imitate him. The text states "us," and while this may include Silas and Timothy, it is most likely a nosism (cf. 1 Thessalonians 1.5-6). Paul often used "our," "we," "us" for himself.[2]

---

[2] See the discussion on "imitation" in 1 Thessalonians 1.

Paul wrote that believers should imitate him not only in adhering to the doctrine he taught, but also in behavior. Behavior is emphasized here. Paul reminded them that when with them he did not "act disorderly," ἠτακτήσαμεν. The verb corresponds with the adjective ἀτάκτως found in verse 6. The meaning of the verb and adjective is one who behaves without discipline, one unruly or idle.

Paul continued in verse 8, reminding them that he paid his own way when with them (cf. 1 Thessalonians 2.9). Paul worked *hard*. The expression is ἐν κόπῳ καὶ μόχθῳ. The noun κόπος mean labor, often attended with trouble. The noun μόχθος is only found in Paul's writings and denotes painful, difficult labor. His work involved working "night and day," νύκτα καὶ ἡμέραν. While trained in manual labor as a tentmaker, Paul had spent most of his adult life as an academic. Earning a living in manual labor must have been a challenge. But throughout his ministry Paul never complained and supplied his own needs. He wrote the Corinthians:

> And we toil, by working with own hands. When we are reviled, we bless; when we are persecuted, we endure (1 Corinthians 4.12).

> And when I was present with you and was in need, I burdened no one. For my need was completely supplied when the brethren came from Macedonia. So I kept and will keep myself from being a burden to you in everything (2 Corinthians 11.9).

If anyone deserved financial support it was Paul, God's handpicked apostle. But he worked tirelessly to present God's gospel of grace and the revelations he received about the Church. Paul avoided demanding wages to set an example, for he did not want to be accused of exploiting congregations for gain. Indeed, in 1 Corinthians 11 and 12 he mocked those he called "super apostles," the arrogant false teachers who charged the Corinthians to teach.

In verse 9, Paul wrote he had authority to demand payment but did not exercise it. Instead, he wished to be an example for imitation. How the Lord changes lives! Was this the same man who had advanced in Judaism and persecuted believers? Trained by one of the great Pharisaic scholars of Judaism, Paul was on the fast track. He was wealthy, esteemed, and may have been the youngest member of the Sanhedrin. Yet he wrote the Philippians:

> [7] But whatever things were gain to me, I have regarded them loss, because of the Christ. [8] But doubtless, I regard all things to be loss because of the superiority of the knowledge of Christ Jesus my Lord, for whom I lost all the things and regard them as dung, so I might gain Christ, [9] and might be found in Him—not having my righteousness, which *is* from Law, but the righteousness from God which *is* through *the* faithfulness of Christ, by the faith, [10] to know Him and the power of His resurrection and *the* fellowship of His sufferings, being conformed to His death, [11] if in some way, I might attain to the out-resurrection from the dead (Philippians 3.7-11).

Like Moses, who saw God face-to-face, Paul saw the risen Lord. As Moses became the humblest man on earth (Numbers 12.3), so Paul. With God, nothing is impossible.

---

[10] For even when we were with you, we kept commanding you, If anyone is not willing to work, do not let him eat.
[11] For we hear some walk among you disorderly, who do not work, but are busybodies.
[12] Now we command and exhort such ones by our Lord Jesus Christ, that they work quietly, so they may eat their own bread.
[13] And you, brethren, should not grow weary doing good. [14] Now if anyone does not obey our word

through this letter, identify this person and do not associate with him so that he might be ashamed.
15 Yet do not regard *him* as *an* enemy but admonish *him* as *a* brother.

Comment:

Verses 10-15: The Thessalonians were a model church but not without problems. No group of believers is. Paul heard that some were acting disorderly, ἀτάκτως, and commanded believers to avoid them (verse 11; cf. verse 6). Some were also not working and had become busybodies, meddling in others' lives. As a result, Paul commanded that if one was unwilling to work, he was not to eat (verse 10). The verb παρηγγέλλομεν is translated "kept commanding" an imperfect active indicative, denoting continuous action. Apparently, this problem required ongoing attention.

Believers are not to be lazy. Laziness and idleness lead to becoming a pest, a nuisance, a gossip, behavior displeasing to God. Paul's statement, "who do not work, but are busybodies," μηδὲν ἐργαζομένους ἀλλὰ περιεργαζομένους, is a pun. The text literally reads, "who do not work but work around." Instead of being useful and productive, they went about doing mischief.

Paul's command about not eating for one unwilling to work should be a rule for all churches and believers. Indeed, it should be a rule for all society. Paul did not instruct if one was *unable* to work but if one was *unwilling* to work. We must help believers unable to work. But churches and fellow believers have no duty to support the able-bodied who refuse to work.

Paul continued in verse 12, commanding and exhorting those who were walking disorderly, not working, and being busybodies, to work quietly so they might eat their own food—food they had earned. Again, Paul gave the command, "by our Lord Jesus Christ," denoting he received this instruction from the risen Lord. The noun translated "quietly," ἡσυχία, is found three other times in the New Testament. Luke used it for the crowd who held their peace when Paul began to speak in Aramaic (Acts 22.2). The other two times, Paul used it regarding women in the local congregation (1 Timothy 2.11-12). The essential sense of the noun is not silence itself but in not interfering or meddling. The noun denoting silence itself is σιγή (cf. Acts 21.40; Revelation 8.1).

In verse 13, Paul encouraged his readers that they "should not grow weary in doing good." Believers live in a fallen world—deceit and dishonesty flourish. We are behind enemy lines, in a world system under Satan's operational control. We are not yet home. God has given us His word and the message of salvation, the world's only true hope. As believers who have come to know the risen Lord, we have the privilege to serve the One who loves us and died for us. As such, we should thankfully and joyfully proclaim God's love and salvation to a lost world. Paul is our example of faithfulness.

In verse 14, Paul repeated his command from verse 6 that if one did not obey his instruction, believers must identify and disassociate with him. The intent was to make such a believer ashamed of his disobedience and behavior. But Paul declared he should not be regarded as an enemy but admonished as a brother (verse 15). Reproof should be firm but with love.

Our company as believers is important. The adage, "birds of a feather, flock together" is true. In most cases, those who associate with persons disobedient to Christ are turned from Christ.

Final Greetings

16 Now may the Lord of the peace Himself give you the peace through everything, in every way. The Lord *be* with you all!
17 The greeting *is* in my own hand, Paul, which is *my* identifier in every letter. Thus, I write:
18 The grace of our Lord Jesus Christ *be* with you all! Amen.

Comment:

Verses 16-18: Paul closed his letter by asking the Lord to give the Thessalonians peace through everything, in every way, and that He might be with them all.

Paul constantly promoted peace and addressed readers with salutations of peace in all his letters (Romans 1.7, 15.13, 33; 1 Corinthians 1.3; 2 Corinthians 1.2; Galatians 1.3, 6.16; Ephesians 1:2, 6.23; Philippians 1.2; Colossians 1.2; 1 Thessalonians 1.1, 5.23; 2 Thessalonians 1.2, 3.16; 1 Timothy 1.2; 2 Timothy 1.2; Titus 1.4; Philemon 1.3).

Paul wrote we have peace with God because of Christ's work:

> Therefore, because we were declared righteous by faith, we have peace with the God through our Lord Jesus Christ (Romans 5.1).
>
> [14] For He is our peace, the One who made both one and broke down the middle wall of the barrier, [15] the hostility, by His flesh, He nullified the Law of the commands in ordinances so He might create the two in Himself into one new man, thus making peace, ... [17] And when He came, He proclaimed good news: peace to you, those far away, and to those near (Ephesians 2.14-15, 17).
>
> And through Him to reconcile everything to Himself because through Him He made peace through the blood of His cross, whether the things on the earth or the things in the heavens (Colossians 1.20).

The Lord Jesus Christ brought peace with God through His own blood. He died for our sins, paying the penalty of death to satisfy God's justice.

Paul declared our God is the God of peace:

> For the God is not of disorder but of peace (1 Corinthians 14.33a).

> Now the God of the peace will soon crush Satan under your feet. The grace of our Lord Jesus Christ *be* with you. Amen (Romans 16.20)!

Interestingly, Paul chose "God of the peace" to describe His crushing Satan. Peace can only come when the source of rebellion and discord is destroyed.

Paul wrote daily peace comes from living under the control of the Holy Spirit and following his teachings:

> But the fruit of the Spirit is love, joy, peace, patience, kindness, goodness, faithfulness (Galatians 5.22).

> And the peace of God, which surpasses all understanding, will guard your hearts and your minds in Christ Jesus (Philippians 4.7).

> What you learned, and received, and heard, and saw in me, practice these things. And the God of the peace will be with you (Philippians 4.9).

> And let the peace of the God rule in your hearts (for which you were also called in one body) and be thankful (Colossians 3.15).

God reveals His message of peace through His servants and that peace is a primary characteristic of His kingdom. Paul declared:

> And how could they preach if they should not be sent? Just as it has been written: How beautiful *are* the feet of those who proclaim peace, of those who proclaim the good things (Romans 10.15)!

> For the kingdom of the God is not food and drink, but righteousness, and peace, and joy in *the* Holy Spirit (Romans 14.17).

Apart from the Lord Jesus Christ there is no peace. Men constantly speak of peace and governments sign peace treaties. But if peace comes, it is fleeting. Christ alone, the Prince of Peace, can bring permanent peace to the human heart. We remain restless until we rest in Him.

Paul's practice was to dictate his letters to a secretary who penned the letter. The exception seems have been Galatians, where he declared, "See with what large letters I wrote you with my own hand" (Galatians 6.11; cf. 1 Corinthians 16.21; Colossians 4.18). Paul had an eye problem which affected his vision which explains why wrote in "large letters," πηλίκοις γράμμασιν (cf. Galatians 4.15).

To thwart forgeries, Paul wrote the last part of his letters with his own hand and ended them with a grace statement (verses 17-18):

> The greeting *is* in my own hand, Paul, which is *my* identifier in every letter. Thus, I write: [18] The grace of our Lord Jesus Christ *be* with you all! Amen.

All Paul's letters (even Hebrews) close with a grace statement. No one declared God's grace more than Paul. He recognized the Lord's wondrous grace to Israel, to Gentiles, and to himself, in that God saved him to be the apostle of the Gentiles (Romans 11.13). As the vanguard of opposition to Christ after His crucifixion, Paul deserved death. But God graciously saved him. He never got over it. He became God's apostle of grace.

Closing Note: 1-2 Thessalonians

The Bible tells a story—an epic of multiple dramas with a cast of men, women, spirit beings, and God Himself. God is its author and chief character. The plot is God's revelation of Himself and His plan. Like all dramas, it has crises, misunderstandings, victories, failures, reversals of fortune, regrets, good, and evil. The Bible is a love story, a tale of God's love for mankind, a tale of ultimate sacrifice. The Bible is a war story, narrating God's war against His enemies, those who hate truth and righteousness. When God fights, He fights to win. While wounded, He utterly crushes His adversaries.

The characters in God's drama have free will, obeying or rebelling against Him. But as every author knows, the actions of the characters end the story as the author intended. Make no mistake, those in God's drama exercise free will. God's genius allows billions of wills to operate and have the story end as the Author planned. Each person is given a choice: ally with God against the powers of darkness or join God's enemies. Choosing wisely means love, joy, peace, and eternal life in God's presence. Choosing unwisely means eternal punishment and separation from God.

To understand God's plan, one must understand and distinguish between His design for Israel and Gentiles, His prophetic plan, and His plan for the Church. Each has a distinct program and destiny.

While some things are learned purely intellectually, deeper knowledge comes through experience. The great lesson from experience is that without God, all is futility, hopelessness, and death.

Isaiah wrote about evil in his generation:

> Woe to them that call evil good, and good evil; that put darkness for light, and light for darkness; that put bitter for sweet, and sweet for bitter (Isaiah 5.20)!

The goal of evil is to normalize perversion and wickedness. God allows mankind to destroy himself and His creation to reveal wickedness. Such freedom demonstrates to the angelic host and humanity life as a result of rebellion against Him.

Most of God's drama is revealed in His prophetic plan that began with His promise in Genesis 3.15, after Adam and Eve's disobedience of eating from the forbidden tree. All mankind was in view at this stage.

After this, God revealed a new chapter of His plan when He made a covenant with Abraham, in whom He created a new race, a covenant people, dividing humanity into Jew and Gentile. Israel became God's vehicle to reveal Himself and His prophetic plan for Israel and the nations (Gentiles).

What is missing? Absent from God's prophetic plan is the Church. According to Abrahamic Covenant, all Gentile blessing would come through the Jews. They were the key to Gentile blessing and fulfillment of God's prophetic plan. If one understands this, one can understand why they, more than other people, have been the focus of oppression and persecution throughout history. Satan knows the Jewish people are the center of gravity of God's prophetic plan. If he can destroy them, God's prophetic plan cannot succeed. Operating behind the curtain, Satan is the source of anti-Semitism. Hidden, he controls governments, which is why the United Nations almost always votes unanimously votes (with the exception of the United States and sometime England) against Israel.

The prophets foretold the Jewish people's rejection of their Messiah. What was unknown, however, was that this rejection would continue for a lengthy period. Peter and the rest of the apostles expected the nation to repent and accept Jesus as the Messiah after He rose from the dead. They thought the Tribulation would occur soon. Why did they think this?

The prophetic writings seemed to indicate that the prophecies about the Messiah would all be fulfilled in a relatively short timeframe after He appeared. Jesus' answer to His disciples in Matthew 24 about end time prophecies seemed to confirm this view.

The apostles remembered His words and His promise that they would sit on twelve thrones ruling Israel's twelve tribes (Matthew 19.28). The last question they asked Him before He ascended was, "Lord, is this the time when you will restore the kingdom to Israel?" (Acts 1.6). His reply was cryptic, a hint that everything might not occur as quickly as they expected. He told them, "It is not for you to know times or seasons that the Father set in place by His own authority" (Acts 1.7). He continued, saying,

> [8] But you will receive power when the Holy Spirit comes on you. And you will be My witnesses in Jerusalem, and in all Judea, and Samaria, and to the ends the earth (Acts 1.8).

They were to await the coming of the Holy Spirit and be Christ's witnesses in Jerusalem, Judea, Samaria, and the rest of the world. This agreed with the prophetic program. But the Scriptures reveal that they never went to the ends of the earth. Why? The Jewish nation refused to repent. As a result, God interrupted His prophetic program.

On the day of Pentecost Peter quoted Joel:

> [17] And it will be in the last days, says the God, I will pour out of My Spirit on all flesh. And your sons and your daughters will prophesy. And your young men will see visions. And your old men will dream dreams. [18] And on My men servants and My women servants in those days, I will pour out of My Spirit, and they will prophesy. [19] And I will give wonders in the heaven above and signs on the earth below—blood and fire and billows of smoke. [20] The sun will be turned into darkness and the moon into blood before the great and glorious Day of *the* Lord comes. [21] And it will be,

> everyone who should call on the name of *the* Lord will be saved (Acts 2.17-21 cf. Joel 2.28-32).

Part of what Peter said was fulfilled—the Holy Spirit came, dreams, visions, and prophesy occurred. Wonders in the heaven, the sun turning to darkness and the moon to blood did not occur. Those events concerned the Tribulation. But Peter quoted all Joel's prophecy for he thought those things would soon occur and Christ would return to set up His earthly kingdom.

Psalm 2 outlines God's prophetic program. It reveals Jewish and Gentile opposition to Christ, God's wrath against earth (the Tribulation), and Christ's rule of the world. The Psalm seemed to indicate everything would be completed in a short period.

Psalm 110.1-2 reads:

> 1 The LORD said to my Lord, Sit at my right hand, until I make your enemies your footstool. 2 The LORD will send the rod of your strength out of Zion: rule in the midst of your enemies.

This prophecy concerns the Lord's ascension and sitting at the Father's right hand until His enemies are conquered at His return. He will then rule earth from Zion (Jerusalem). No break in these events is noted. Where are we now prophetically? For the moment, God's prophetic program is static. The Lord remains seated at His Father's right hand after two millennia.

Psalm 118.22 reads,

> The stone which the builders refused is become the head stone of the corner.

This prophecy was fulfilled when the Jews rejected and crucified Christ. Has He become the headstone of the corner? No. This will occur when Israel repents and accepts Him as their Messiah and King. When they do, He will establish His earthly kingdom and rule. The prophecy seemed to indicate everything would occur in a short timeframe.

Isaiah wrote:

> [6] For to us a child is born, to us a son is given: and the government will be on his shoulder: and his name will be called Wonderful, Counsellor, The mighty God, The everlasting Father, The Prince of Peace. [7] Of the increase of his government and peace there will be no end, on the throne of David, and on his kingdom, to order it, and to establish it with judgment and with justice from henceforth even forever. The zeal of the LORD of hosts will perform this (Isaiah 9.6-7).

Verse 6a was fulfilled with Christ's birth. Is the government, verse 6b, now on Christ's shoulders? Is He ruling earth from Jerusalem? Is His government increasing? Is the world ruled justly? Again, the passage reads as if everything follows in short order. No long gap between the events is evident.

> [1] The Spirit of the Lord GOD is on me; because the LORD has anointed me to preach good tidings to the meek; he has sent me to bind up the brokenhearted, to proclaim liberty to the captives, and the opening of the prison to them that are bound; [2] To proclaim the acceptable year of the LORD, and the day of vengeance of our God; to comfort all that mourn (Isaiah 61.1-2)

Verses 1 and 2a were fulfilled at the Lord's first coming (Luke 4.16-21). Verse 2b and 2c remain unfilled—the day of vengeance, the Tribulation, the day of comfort, the kingdom. The prophecy seemed to indicate everything would happen together.

Zechariah wrote:

> [9] Rejoice greatly, O daughter of Zion; shout, O daughter of Jerusalem: behold, your King comes to you: he is just, and having salvation; lowly, and riding on an ass, and on a colt the foal of an ass. [10] And

> I will cut off the chariot from Ephraim, and the horse from Jerusalem, and the battle bow will be cut off: and he will speak peace to the heathen: and his dominion will be from sea even to sea, and from the river even to the ends of the earth (Zechariah 9.9-10).

Verse 9 was fulfilled on Palm Sunday. Verse 10 describes the Lord's victory at Armageddon and the establishment of His earthly kingdom. It remains unfulfilled. No time gap is apparent in the prophecy.

Luke wrote:

> 31 And behold, you will conceive in *the* womb and will give birth to *a* son. And you will call His name Jesus. 32 He will be great and will be called Son of the Highest. And the Lord God will give Him the throne of His father, David (Luke 1.31-32).

Verses 31 and 32a were fulfilled. Jesus was born of Mary. Has verse 32a been fulfilled? Is Jesus seated on David's throne in Jerusalem? It will be fulfilled after Jesus returns and sets up His kingdom. Again, no indication of a time gap exists between these events.

What are we to make of these verses? Were the apostles wrong? Did they misunderstand the prophets? The Lord's words and the apostles understanding assumed the Jewish nation would accept their Messiah. Jesus knew this would not happen but had to let everything play out, to let man's free will operate. He gave the nation an opportunity to repent and accept Him and told them the condition of His return:

> 37 Jerusalem, Jerusalem, the one who kills the prophets and stones the ones who have been sent to her! How often I wished to gather your children, as *a* hen gathers her chicks under her wings, and you would not!
> 38 Behold, your house is left to you desolate!
> 39 For I tell you, you should never see Me from now until you should say, Blessed *is*

> the One who comes in *the* name of *the* Lord (Matthew 23.37-39).

Since Jewish nation refused to repent and say, "Blessed is the One who comes in the name of the Lord" after His crucifixion and resurrection, God halted His prophetic program. Jesus' generation was like Moses' generation who refused to believe God and enter the promised land. They wandered the desert forty years and died. The next generation, under Joshua, believed God and entered the land. Jesus' generation was tested forty years and died by Titus' legions in 70 A.D. Throughout the Scriptures, forty is a number for a time of testing. The Jews of Jesus' generation failed but a future generation will meet the succeed—they are the "other sheep" of John 10.16. They will repent and believe Jesus is the Christ and see God's promises fulfilled.

As a result of Israel's national failure, they could not assume God's intended destiny for them to bless Gentiles. But God in His grace had another plan, planned in eternity, He had kept hidden. God would bless Gentiles, not by Israel's *obedience* but by Israel's *disobedience*. Instead of initiating His wrath, the Tribulation, God saved Saul of Tarsus and turned His greatest enemy into His greatest apostle, the apostle of the Gentiles (Romans 11.13).

Paul assumed the mantle of Israel's destiny to become proxy Israel as the light of the Gentiles (Acts 13.43-48; cf. Isaiah 42.6, 49.6), a priest to the Gentiles (Romans 15.15-16; cf. Exodus 19.6; Isaiah 61.6), and a minister of the New Covenant (2 Corinthians 3.4-6; cf. Jeremiah 31.31). As a Jew, Paul could fulfill these roles individually in accord with the Abrahamic Covenant. He could serve as a priest, not as a Levite, but in the role every Jew will have in the kingdom (cf. Micah 4.2; Zechariah 8.20-23). When Christ establishes His earthly kingdom, every Jew who enters the kingdom (all believers) will fulfill the roles of light, priests, and ministers of the New Covenant.

How does 1-2 Thessalonians fit with this?

God's call of Abraham began the creation of a new race, a covenant people. His action divided humanity into Jew and Gentile. God acted similarly with Paul. His calling of Paul created a new race, a third group, the Church, the body of Christ. This is the theological state of the world today, composed of Jew, Gentile, and Church.

What is the Church, the body of Christ? The Church is a *new creation*, neither Jew or Gentile, with Christ as its Head. One becomes a member of the Church by believing Paul's gospel, Christ died for one's sins and rose from the dead. Former identities as Jew or Gentile are shed. In addition, one is indwelt by the Holy Spirit, becomes "in Christ," given eternal life, forgiveness of sins, and identified in Christ's death and resurrection.

The reader should ponder this definition. Was anything like this ever revealed before Paul? One can search the Scriptures, Old Testament, Gospels, letters of James, Peter, John, and Jude and find nothing like it, nothing of the Church, the body of Christ. It was entirely *new*, a *secret*, a divine revelation God gave Paul alone. This is why the Church and all its doctrines are found only in Paul's letters.

The books of the Old Testament, the Gospels, Paul's letter of Hebrews, the letters of James, Peter, John, and Jude concern two groups, Jew and Gentile which concern God's prophetic program. The Church, a new creation, neither Jew nor Gentile, is outside God's prophetic program. Since 1 and 2 Thessalonians is addressed to the Church, the body of Christ, it is outside God's prophetic program. Thus, for God to restart His prophetic program, the Church *cannot* be present. God *must* remove it. This is the essential truth and doctrine of Paul's first two letters.

Since the Church was a secret, the Pre-Tribulation Rapture was a secret. As the Church cannot be found in the Old Testament, Gospels, letters of James, Peter, John, or Jude, the Rapture cannot be found in them either. It can be found only in Paul's letters.

Paul thought God would complete the Church in his lifetime and then initiate the Tribulation. Christ would then return and establish His earthly kingdom. But because of Israel's rebellion (which God knew would continue) this did not occur. God reveals *what* He will do but not *when* He will do it (cf. Acts 1.7). The Church has continued nearly two millennia. We do not know when God will finish it but we are close. God will then complete His prophetic program.

Since Paul thought the Lord would soon complete His Church, he taught the doctrine of the Pre-Tribulation Rapture to the Thessalonians immediately after they believed the gospel. His letters about the Rapture followed shortly, to fortify his teaching and assure them they would not undergo God's wrath in the Tribulation.

Paul wrote Titus that the Pre-Tribulation Rapture was the Church's "blessed hope."

> [11] For the saving grace of the God was revealed to all men, [12] by teaching us that because we denied the ungodliness and the worldly desires, we should live wisely, and righteously, and godly in the present age, [13] as we wait for the blessed hope and appearing of the glory of the great God, even our Savior, Jesus Christ, [14] who gave Himself for us, so He might redeem us from all lawlessness and might purify to Himself *a* special people, eager for good works (Titus 2.11-14).

Resurrection Day for members of the Church is the Rapture, the day God resurrects our bodies and gives us immortal, eternal bodies, to live forever with the Lord Jesus Christ. What glory!

If the reader keeps God's prophetic program for Jew and Gentile separated from God's new program of the Church, he will understand the Scriptures. Confusion and seeming contradictions will cease. Let it be!

About the Author

The author earned his Th.M. degree from Dallas Theological Seminary, majoring in Semitics and Old Testament Studies. Articles he has written are at doctrine.org.

Author's Books

God's Programs: An Introduction to Understanding the Bible
Paul: Apostle of Secrets
The New Testament Study Bible (BDV)
Understanding the Jewish Writings: An Examination of Hebrews, James, 1-2 Peter, 1-3 John, Jude, and Revelation

Good News

The bad news is all have sinned and fall short of God's glory (Romans 3.23). The good news is God has solved the problem of sin and death and gives eternal life to all who want it (Romans 6.23). God showed His love when He sent His Son to die for our sins and pay sin's penalty, death. Because He did all the work, all one can do for salvation is accept His work, believe Christ died for your sins and rose from the dead. The clearest message of salvation is the following:

> 1 Now I declare to you, brethren, the gospel that I proclaimed to you, which you also received, by which also you stand, 2 through which also you are saved, if you possess that message I proclaimed to you, unless you believed in vain. 3 For I delivered to you first what I also received: Christ died for our sins, according to the Scriptures, 4 and that He was buried, and that He has been raised on the third day, according to the Scriptures (1 Corinthians 15.1-4).

Anyone who wishes can know God, have His forgiveness, eternal life, and be with Him forever. If this is your desire, tell God you trust in Christ's death, burial, and resurrection for you. Trust Him. It is that simple.

Made in the USA
Las Vegas, NV
24 March 2023

69631858R00092